MILITARIA
Collecting Print and Manuscript

"THE EMPIRE ON WHICH THE SUN NEVER SETS"

Militaria

Collecting Print and Manuscript

A. H. Denney

A Balfour / Planned Action Book, printed and published by
Photo Precision Ltd., St. Ives, Huntingdon, England

FIRST EDITION 1973

ISBN 0 85936 009 1

Foreword

This is a book for the collector. But unlike many of today's books on collecting it is not for the wealthy man who is looking for an investment against inflation or for the connoisseur of rarities and unique pieces, though in a way many of the pieces shown here are unique. It is essentially a book for the enthusiast who enjoys a hobby which is interesting, instructive, economical and enjoyable. The illustrations are suggestions of the sort of thing that may be sought with real hope of a find and the text is intended to suggest the way that further research might go. I am grateful to Mr. Charles A. Fox for material from the Artists' Rifles and to Mr Ian Morley-Clarke for the originals of some of the illustrations. I am also most grateful to the photographer and the publishers who have taken great pains with the production.

The Author

Country parson, educationalist, writer and collector, Anthony Denney is a graduate of London and Cambridge. His training is in history and he has published some research work on medieval documents. From an early age he has collected books and manuscripts and he firmly believes that we all need a hobby and preferably one which will enable us to learn more about people both past and present.

Contents

Introduction

In the last decade or so we have witnessed a new era in collecting. Almost anything is collectable and a glance around the stock-in-trade of antique and curio shops shows that almost anything is saleable. Whether things are collected for their value or their interest makes little difference, the incentive to collect is a strong one and nostalgia and curiosity are the most prevalent motives. Two wars have impressed on us the extraordinary capacity that we have for destroying things so that it is refreshing to discover that we also have a capacity for preserving the past.

The preservation of things that are beautiful and rare has gone on throughout man's history; but today this is the expensive privilege of the few who can afford it. The collecting of trivial things that have something of past history about them but are not necessarily beautiful, though they are becoming rare, is a hobby in which anyone can indulge without putting himself in 'Queer-Street'. So today there are ardent collectors of coins, medals, stamps, military uniforms, weapons, badges and buttons; history surrounds these things and it is in this worthy company that the collector of military ephemera will find himself at home.

The Oxford Dictionary defines ephemeral as 'lasting only for a day'. This is indeed its correct root meaning, but the figurative use of the word has been extended to describe things 'short lived or transitory', and it is in this sense that we use it here. The things that we are about to describe are, by their very nature, preserved more by good luck than good judgement, more by chance than intention. Most of them were intended to serve a particular purpose and then to be discarded. For some of them their lifetime could have been as long as the period of a man's service in the armed forces or as short a time as it took to receive a letter through the post. All have certain common features – they are written or printed (or both) – they relate to matters military, in peace or war – they are obtainable by you or I if we are prepared for the search and are not the confidential contents of unit offices or the unique items that would ordinarily be found only in a museum – they seldom cost more than a fiver a piece and often only a few pence. For the sake of convenience I have included among them such collectable things as books and prints.

One of the things that makes the collecting of ephemera such an enjoyable hobby is the simple fact that one has no idea what is going to turn up next or where. For example, the picture that is shown on the cover of this book just had to be bought. The superb colouring of the whole thing made it attractive regardless of the subject matter. It was undoubtedly an excellent example of nostalgia for a vanished age getting to work, but when the scene at the bottom was examined – The Grand Review of the Troops at Agra – its place in a collection of military items was assured. Its discovery was impossible to forecast and if a dealer kindly inquired 'what sort of thing are you looking for?' it would have been impossible to have dreamed up a description of anything like this; a jumble sale revealed a printed silk souvenir of the Eighth Army, produced in Egypt for troops to send home to their wives and mothers; a search by a long-suffering and aged relative turned up some records associated with the Franco-Prussian War. Surprise, pleasure, research, a constantly increasing knowledge of past history and people – these are the rewards of this pursuit.

SPECIALISATION

The wealth of material of all sorts that can be found may suggest that sooner or later the collector will be compelled to specialise in one field or another of his subject. The only drawback to specialisation is the eventual increase in the price that will have to be paid for each item. But this need not deter the collector who has an eye to the eventual cash value of his collection. The specialised collection is almost always a more valuable asset than the general.

Obvious classification of material by subject and by date suggests areas for the specialist. Individual regiments, particular campaigns, periods of history, geographical theatres of action: India, Africa etc., personalities: Napoleon, Wellington, kinds of material, prisoners of war, philatelic or postal history, are all possibilities. World War I obviously constitutes one immense source of material of all sorts, still reasonably easy to obtain. As we go back in history the type of available material changes. Postcards of the Boer War are still occasionally found, photos are still relatively easy. The Franco-Prussian War and the Crimea are much more difficult, but manuscript material, letters, diaries, postal stationery, newspapers, books, periodicals and prints are not too difficult to discover. The Napoleonic wars again are not too easy in terms of variety, but they covered a relatively long period and there is an immense literature dealing with them. Newspapers of the period turn up quite often, prints and books are also frequently found. Letters are naturally scarce, but often a collection not necessarily military in origin may contain references to contemporary events. This can be an expensive period because of its long-standing popularity and so will appeal to the collector prepared to spend rather more generously than those preferring later periods of history.

We need to remember that military history is being made all the time. World War II is slipping into historical perspective but is a very prolific source of material which is still readily and cheaply available. The problem is to discriminate between the scarce and the common items. Although millions were issued, ration books of war time date are becoming very scarce. Propaganda publications, leaflets and posters are even scarcer. Personal documents are still in the hands of men and women who served in the forces if they have not already been thrown away. Newspapers of the war years are still very common but it is anybody's guess how long they will remain so! Much material is still in private houses and has not yet got into the dealers' hands so here is a chance to search among your friends before they clear it out as rubbish.

Whether you decide to specialise or just jog along picking up whatever comes, it is a fascinating and informative pastime and I wish you joy.

Plate I(a) Cover from Durban to Prisoner of War Camp at Diyatalawa, Ceylon.

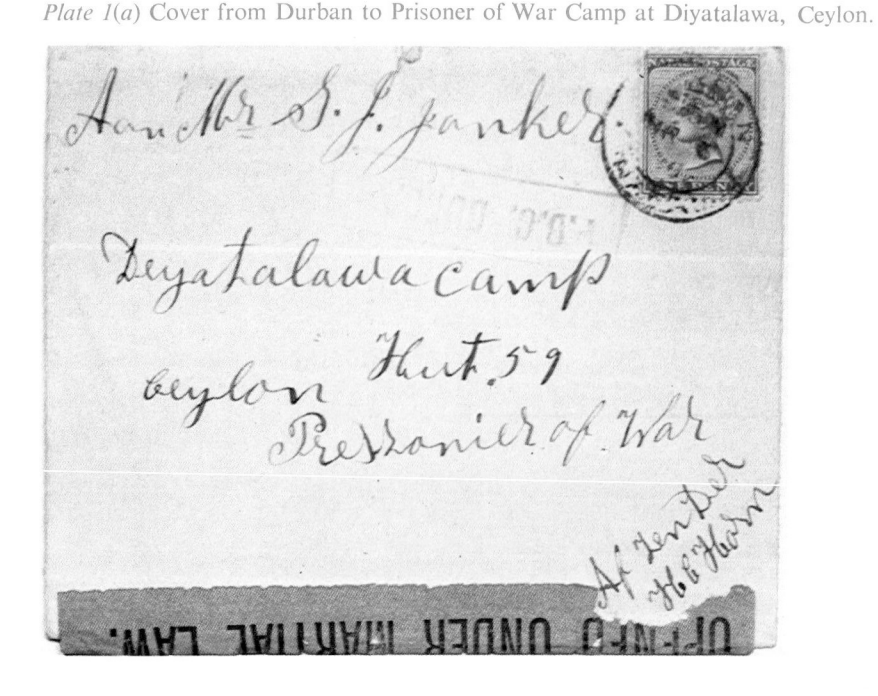

Military Postal History

Postal history is a most important part of phila-tely and is consequently both well documented and commercially organised. Of all aspects of military ephemera it is probably the one most actively pursued. Items of postal history are readily available in the auction rooms and through dealers and are increasing in price year by year; but the military side of postal history is still a happy hunting ground for the enthusiast, both general collector and specialist. Dealers are helpful and interested and fine examples of postal markings are available at reasonable prices. Scarce markings of minor campaigns can be relatively costly, but even these are within the range of most collectors and always have the great consolation of marketability and increased value as time goes by.

Four sorts of material are worth looking for, and these can be subdivided into several separate categories.

1. Pre-stamp letters or covers bearing cancel-lations or marks indicating a military origin.

These will cover the period up to 1840 and therefore, from the military point of view, the Low Countries campaign of 1743, in which postal markings were for the first time applied to soldiers' mail, viz a simple AB in a circle; the Dutch Campaign of 1799, in which the British Post Office for the first time supervised the col-lection and delivery of mail in the field, marking it with a crown and the words Army Bag; the Peninsular War, in which soldiers' mail was routed via Lisbon and marked with the stamp of the British Post Office there; and the Napoleonic wars, in which there seem to have been no specific postal markings from abroad but did produce a Prisoners of War stamp on letters from prisoners interned in Great Britain. This stamp originated from the Transport Office at Chatham. All these markings are scarce and not very easy to find but

Plate 1(b) Postcard from Sofia during the First Balkan War.

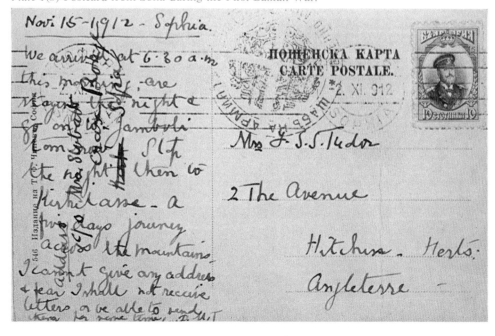

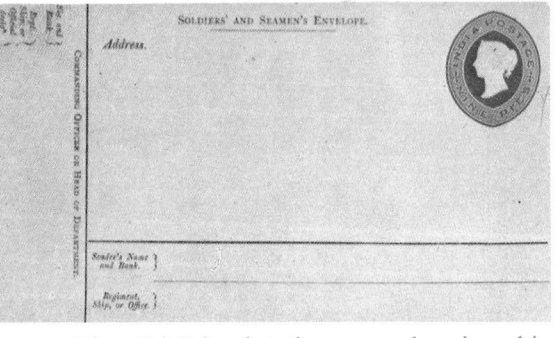

Plate 2(a) Printed stationery envelope issued in 1879 for the use of the armed forces in India.

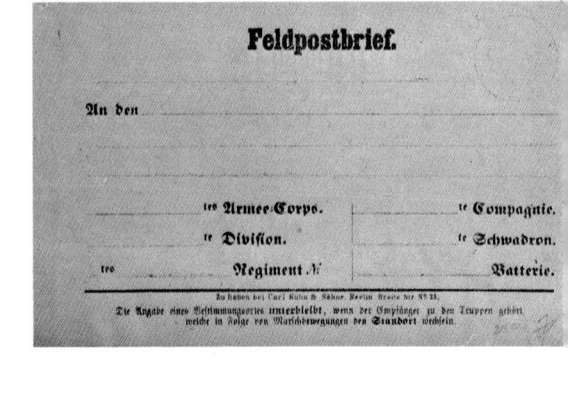

Plate 2(b) Field Post envelope as used by German units in the period of the Franco-Prussian War.

there are a number of foreign markings of the same period originating from the continent which widens the area of search. It is also worth looking at the seals used and manuscript markings which indicate origin, but these are mentioned in our remarks on letters.

2. Mail bearing adhesive stamps, which were cancelled with obliterations, which reveal the military origin of the mail.

The first major campaign from which comes mail with identifiable cancellations is the Crimean War of 1854–55. During this war Army Post Offices operated in Constantinople, Varna and Balaclava and there were sub-offices elsewhere. Special postmarks with crown and stars or O x O were used from the Crimea. Some letters however were brought direct to London and were cancelled at the Foreign Branch Office there before distribution. These carry a numbered cancellation from 45 to 49.

Coming to more recent times the Boer War offers a quantity of postal material which is readily obtainable. Covers and cards bear several different types of markings in addition to the cancellations. These latter are easily identifiable as they state their origin. Most are circular marks carrying the words Field Post Office British Army South Africa or Army Post Office South Africa; they also carry the date in the centre. Censor marks are also common and labels indicating that they have been opened under martial law. Prisoners of war were held in Bermuda and Ceylon and elsewhere beyond the field of battle and the camps have their special hand-stamps; one of the commonest is Diyatalawa Camp, Ceylon. Town cancellations on British postage stamps with the appropriate dates will also be from army sources.

The war broke out in October 1899 and a post office was soon established at Cape Town. The end of hostilities came on May 31st 1902, so there was a fairly long period covered by the cancellations. Mail bearing marks during this period other than military marks or cancellations needs to be examined for content as often army matters are referred to which are of interest, also military

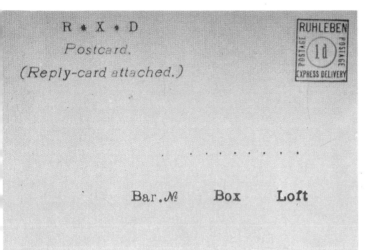

Plate 3 (a) & (b) Postal stationery used in Ruhleben Camp.

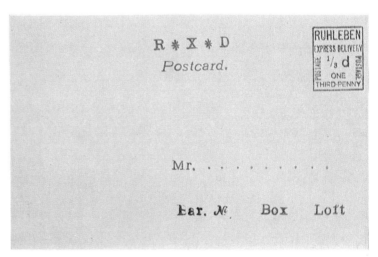

Plates 4 (a) & (b) show printed stationery in use after the suppression of the camp service.

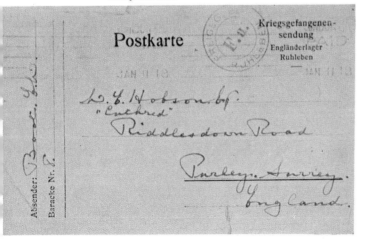

Plate 4 (b)

Plate 5(a) Printed stationery
for use by Prisoners
of War in Germany.

Plate 5(b) A Field Post card adapted
for Prisoner of War use.
World War I.

personnel may have used normal postal channels for their correspondence. For example a Cape of Good Hope letter card, dated December 11th 1899 and cancelled Observatory Road C.G.H., was in fact written from Maitland Camp and the correspondent writes "I have given everybody the news I can think of and it gets a bit off writing several letters in a tent . . ." The letter was to an address in Lincoln, England.

3. Ordinary mail carrying no adhesive stamps but franked with a military post office cancel.

This group comprises much of the mail of the last two wars, but overlaps with the next group of printed stationery which also carries the same frankings.

It is in World War I that the unstamped mail which then became the norm becomes really prolific in quantity. During the Boer War stamps were not always available and covers turn up quite often with this fact noted by the sender. But from 191₊ the Army Post Office, with free facilities for soldiers in many different theatres of war, operated until the end of September 1920. The cancellations used follow a fairly consistent pattern; single or double circles without identifying numerals were occasionally used at first but Field Post Office numbers appear on most strikes. The procedure for outgoing mail was that all letters for troops abroad were collected in London for shipment to Base Army Post Offices across the channel, thence to the A.P.O's at Divisional Headquarters for distribution to the Units. The numerals used on the strikes refer to the Divisional H.Q's; the letters that sometimes precede the numbers provide in many cases indications of the campaign or geography of the Division, e.g. P B for North Russia and L for Italy.

After 1918 the Rhineland occupation force continued to have the privilege of free mail until 1929.

Plate 6(a)&(b) British printed stationery for use by Prisoners of War in Great Britain during World War II.

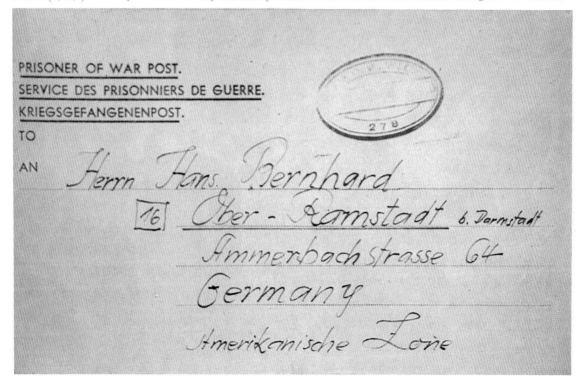

Plate 7(b) German Air Field Post envelope with
special air stamp issued on April 24th
1942.

Plate 7(a) Cover used in World
War II.
The Active Service
Envelope, Army Form
W3078.

Plate 6(b)

The same sort of procedure was used during World War II and Field Post Office strikes with numerals are very common. There were nearly a thousand between 1939 and 1950 and the majority have been located.

4. Specially printed postal stationery for use by the armed forces in the field, by prisoners of war or by organisations supplying benefits to the troops, especially the Red Cross. This latter category is not of course a responsibility of the Post Office, and is therefore not philatelically as interesting as the others.

The Green Active Service envelope (AFW3078) was produced for the troops in the 1914–18 war. They seem to have appeared first in 1915 and although the general pattern remained the same throughout both World Wars, details changed from time to time. Colour of paper used for printing, small variations in wording and, in 1944, a variation in design, provide a good field for the collector.

Field Service Postcards (AFA2042) were used, first with a penny stamp printed on the card.

These were issued before postage charges were remitted for active service personnel. They date from August 12th 1914.

There were many variations of postcards and printed stationery for use in various theatres of war, and only by careful search can the extent of the issues be known. Printed stamped stationery is listed, though not as completely as one would wish, in the books listed at the end of this chapter. Unstamped stationery both British and Foreign is legion and the most profitable field for the collector is the cancellation rather than the format of the card. But there is research to be done in this field and good luck to any who wish to take it on.

Another most interesting collection of printed stationery is that used by Prisoners of War. This comes both stamped and unstamped. A scarce item is the 2½d blue letter sheet issued in 1941. There was also an official postcard issued on November 1st 1942 and marked Post Free; this was W.D., P.M.G. Form No. 6–1. Later envelopes and letter sheets were issued for the use of prisoners, printed in two or three languages.

Mail coming from Germany and used by prisoners of different nationalities in enemy hands forms a most interesting area for collectors. This is particularly so for World War I in which one of the most interesting prisoner of war camps was that at Ruhleben. The story of this camp has been written by J. D. Ketchum in *Ruhleben: a Prison Camp Society*. It was established in 1915 on the Ruhleben racecourse in the Charlottenburg area of Berlin and it organised its own postal service until it was suppressed by the authorities in May 1916. The illustrations tell the story.

Prisoner of War mail to and from the Japanese theatre of war in World War II is very scarce; very little seems to have got through to the prisoners but much was kept in Japanese hands and has come on the market since the war.

In addition to the Field Post Offices and Prisoner of War camps there is a variety of material for those interested in war time mail.

Recently, interest has been aroused by the Air-graphs of World War II. These were introduced in order to speed up delivery of forces' mail and enable post to be carried by air at vastly less cost and trouble than through the normal letter or card. Special forms were available to servicemen which, when completed, were photographed. On arrival at destination a 5"×4" print was made and was placed in a special window envelope for delivery. A role of microfilm weighing about 4oz could contain as many as 1500 messages.

Christmas greeting cards of all sorts were produced both by and for the forces serving overseas in both the Wars. Both types are illustrated. Among the most attractive were silk embroidered cards of World War I. These were made by French women and sold to the troops for dispatch home. Some are simple decorative designs, some have a corps badge and some have a pocket in which was placed a small card on which a message could be written. These silk cards are still quite easy to find

Plate 9 (a) Illustrated postcard used by English and German troops during World War I.

Plate 9 (b) Illustrated postcard used by English and German troops during World War I.

Plate 10(a) Behind the Sandbags.

Plate 10(b) English soldiers escorting German prisoners for shipment to England.

Plate 11(a) One of our Monster Guns.

and not yet very expensive, but scarcity is driving up the price.

Since 1945 there have been a variety of locations where British troops have been stationed and where the Post Office has operated, Aden, the Korean War of 1950–54, Southern Arabia and stations in Africa.

Attention naturally tends to focus upon the British Army and campaigns in which British forces have been engaged. But there are of course many other wars and campaigns of which postal records are available. The Franco-Prussian War of 1870–1 produced the famous balloon post whereby the besieged Parisians flew mail by balloon out of the city and over the heads of the Prussian troops. The Boxer Rebellion of 1901 produced a variety of national mails from the besieged legations in Peking. The French Revolution, if the collector is ambitious, offers opportunity for records of the Revolutionary Army in its struggle with the anti-revolutionary coalitions of Europe. In the later campaigns of the French armies in Europe, Departments were set up in occupied territories and each had its postal handstamp. Items of this sort tend to be expensive and scarce but can be found by a careful search of auction catalogues.

During the last few years enterprising dealers have latched on to the popularity of commemorative covers. These are frequently issued in series to commemorate events in military, air or naval history. A finely illustrated cover is designed and a special handstamp applied to the normal postage rate adhesive. A certain number of covers of a particular issue may carry signatures of persons actually involved or associated with events commemorated within the period of the last war or later. These carry a premium on the normal purchase price. While admiring the style and design of these covers one must admit a slight misgiving about their place in a collection of military ephemera. Apart from the signed copies they are

Plate 11(b) A London Heavy Battery in Action.

104.
Official Photograph—Crown Copyright reserved

A London Heavy Battery in action
"Daily Mail" War Pictures

not in the same category as original covers of a campaign, and even the signed copies are to some extent a contrived memorial separated from the event itself by many years. However if carefully used in association with original material they are a very useful and colourful addition to an exhibition page or album layout. The illustrations on the covers are reproductions of original prints or depict uniforms or arms of regiments and are tastefully chosen and well produced. They, therefore, might reasonably take their place among a collection of prints and illustrations.

Prices

Prices of philatelic material of good quality tend to be relatively high. Philately is a long-standing and popular hobby and, like so many such 'collecting' hobbies, has been used as a means of investment to offset inflation as well as a matter of personal interest. Specialist dealers charge in proportion to their expert knowledge, reputation and quality of material, general dealers frequently have good items but do not profess to be specialists in postal history and pass material at rather lower prices and often prefer to sell in lots. The

Plate 12(a) Au Revoir - not Good-Bye

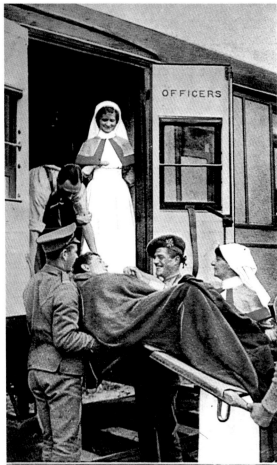

Plate 12(b) A case for 'Blighty'.

A CASE FOR "BLIGHTY"   CANADIAN OFFICIAL

purchaser of a lot can often remove the item he particularly wants and send the rest back to auction to offset his original outlay. This requires some careful checking of auction lots, but is a very usual and economic way of buying.

Twentieth century items, apart from rarities, should not cost more than about £5 a piece at the most and many Field Post Office cancellations, censor marks, and printed stationery of both world wars are readily available as low as 50p an item. The Boer War is getting more difficult and items of any sort are not easy below £3 each and may rise to £7–£8 each according to the quality and scarcity of the markings.

The Franco-Prussian War of 1870–71 will cost £3 to £5 for regimental cachets and used printed stationery with regimental marks. Balloon post items may be as low as £5 but more likely to be around £10. As we go back in the nineteenth century, particularly the smaller campaigns, items tend to be between £5 and £10. But these are generally specialist prices and do not preclude the occasional lucky find. However, this material is becoming increasingly scarce and prices are unlikely to fall. Expenditure on a good clean item with clear markings indicating date, unit, F.P.O., camp or other source, will always be worthwhile and the collector may rest assured of a good investment and worthwhile swap item if his interests change.

Plate 13(a) Sentimental cards from England.

MY HEART'S IN MY HOMELAND (3).

I remember the old folks I loved there, who sat in the old-
fashioned room,
I remember the words that were falling, the hands that I
clasped in the gloom;
There are lands far away proud and lovely, there are home-
steads more stately and fair,
But I'm longing to see all the dear folks again—'tis heaven
for me over there!

Plate 13 (b) Sentimental cards from England.

With my Love.

It seems the world goes smoother,
And it kind of makes you smile,
When you know that though you're absent,
You're remembered all the while.

Plate 14 (*a*) Examples of sentiment from France.

Plate 14 (*b*) Examples of sentiment from France.

Plate 15 (*a*) & (*b*) Examples of sentiment
from France.

Plate 16 (*a*) Italian – Second World War card

The Picture Postcard

Postcards are a recent means of communication and from the point of view of the collector of military ephemera cover the period from the Boer War onwards. Nevertheless, they are about the most prolific and the cheapest item of which he can avail himself. There are, of course, scarce items worthy of a good hunt but at present prices are still very reasonable and there is an immense variety to choose from. The first nation to use the postcard was Austria and the first postcard was issued there on October 1st 1869. Britain followed exactly a year later. The first picture postcards appeared during the Franco-Prussian War and were produced by an enterprising stationer in a small village named Besnardeau. The French troops in the district wanted a simple means of communicating with their families and the stationer saved them the trouble of writing letters which required paper and envelopes by selling them cards decorated with stacked arms, cannons and various designs expressing patriotic sentiment. These cards are scarce and are a considerable stage removed from the picture postcards which became so popular at the close of the century and throughout the period up to and including the First World War.

On September 1st 1894 privately printed postcards for use with adhesive stamps were officially allowed in Britain and it was in this year that Messrs. George Stewart of Edinburgh and F. T. Corkett of Leicester began the production of the first British picture postcards. In spite of a slow start, postcards really seized upon the imagination of the British people, and after the turn of the century became a craze which reflected every possible aspect of life, scenery and sentiment that could be dreamed up by the printers and collectors.

Plate 16 (b) Italian – Second World War Card

AFTER A DAY'S
MARCH
THEY FEEL AS HEAVY
AS THIS. 'PON MY SOLE!

The Boer War began in 1899 and was an apt subject for patriotic cards. An artist already known for his contributions to the illustrated magazines, Richard Caton Woodville, was responsible for a number of the early cards which showed troops in action and army types in uniform. The card we have illustrated here combines illustration with photography and is a product of George Stewart of Edinburgh. Although the use of the address side of the card for messages was allowed after 1897 printers still left room on the picture side for this purpose and the practice of surrounding the picture with writing continued well into the next century. The war in South Africa engendered a spate of cards which sprang from the interest in the armed forces both at home and overseas. There were series depicting historic as well as contemporary uniform. The war was also an occasion to introduce the 'news' card.

Plate 17 (a) & (b) Humorous cards - First and Second World Wars.

GIVE 'EM SOCKS

"IT'LL SOON BE HANGING ON THE SIEGFRIED LINE!"

Just as early in the nineteenth century local and national events were recorded by the engraver who was the journalist for the less literate of his contemporaries, so the postcard in both photograph and drawing provided an economical record of events. Returning troops and civic welcomes were represented and no doubt sold well to the participants; there were also the great events of the war itself, Luck's card of the relief of Mafeking and Ladysmith were among the firm's most popular issues.

Plate 18 Embroidered cards.

My Best Kisses

The interest in military things, once begun, continued beyond the conclusion of the Boer War and regimental uniforms and groups, often accompanied by brief notes of regimental history, became popular. The chief producers of such cards were Luck, always in the field with individual cards and series, Stewart and Woolf, and Gale and Polden. The last named firm was based

Sweet Remembrance

GOOD LUCK

at Aldershot and so catered for the troops there and had ample opportunity for obtaining material which was both topical and accurate.

Between the Boer War and World War I there were several events that deserved and received attention from the postcard illustrators. The British Alliance with Japan, the Russo-Japanese War, the Boxer Rebellion, European troubles, particularly in the Balkans, all gave rise to illustrations or photographs of personalities. The Boxer Rebellion produced some attractively printed cards from China. The illustration often occupied only half the picture side, the rest being left for the message; such cards are often more valuable for their postal cancellations than their illustrations.

Plate 19 Embroidered cards.

WORLD WAR I

The Golden Age of the picture postcard is generally regarded as ending with the introduction of the 1d rate for cards on June 3rd 1918. Thus the first World War marks for many collectors the last period in which postcards retain real interest.

Certainly the war provides every imaginable type of card and they have the present merit of still being readily and cheaply obtainable. Before 1914 sentiments of patriotism and military valour occupied the talents of most artists employed by the producers when they were depicting anything but regimental uniforms or the like. The tradition continued in the early stages of the war, but as time went on and the true nature of the conflict became apparent a different mood was reflected in the cards. Many series, both English and French, depict the destruction brought about by

DARING DEEDS.

ACTING-SERGT. W. WINTER (Distinguished Conduct Medal),
1st Royal Berkshire Regt.

For conspicuous gallantry on November 2nd, when he left
his trench at great risk and recovered a machine gun which
had been buried by a shell. He then worked the gun by
himself, the officer and man previously manning it having
been wounded.

DARING DEEDS.

PTE. C. HARFORD (Distinguished Conduct Medal),
15th Hussars.

For conspicuously gallant conduct on October 27th and 28th,
when, acting as a despatch rider near Veldhoek, he carried
five messages to the firing line, during which period he had
two horses killed and one wounded.

MISS EDITH CAVELL
MURDERED
October 12th 1915

REMEMBER!

Plate 20 Propaganda cards produced in England.

shelling and some of the rigours and horrors of trench warfare.

One of the most popular series of cards was that issued by the Daily Mail. In 1916 the newspaper obtained exclusive rights to the reproduction of photographs taken by official photographers on the Western front. Because these were actual photographs of men engaged in battle as well as many ordinary military routines, they brought to those at home a sense of realism and personal involvement, only equalled by today's television broadcasts. People who looked at the cards could sometimes recognise someone of their own in the scenes shown. They were printed in millions in both black and white and colour and they were immensely popular. The cards sold in sets of eight for sixpence and special albums were available to hold them. At least twenty-two sets were issued.

The Daily Mail cards, though the most popular, were not the only ones which came from on the spot sources. A series entitled 'Official photograph showing British Advance in the West' were issued by the Sport and General Press Agency, the photographs being taken by permission of the C-in-C of the B.E.F. Though less numerous than the Daily Mail series they depict the horrors of war with equal intensity.

Cards of similar type were produced by French publishers in black and white and in sepia. Most of these depict the devastation of town and countryside, the destruction of buildings, churches and civic monuments. Others show troop movements, embarkations, and train loadings. One series shows a before and after scene and is marked

Plate 21(b) A Raphael Tuck 'Empire' postcard.

Plate 21(a) South African War Post Card.

Plate 22 Postcards produced in France showing war damage and scenes of troop movements.

on the message side 'Passed by Censor'. Several of the French cards have their titles in English and French and obviously had a big sale among the troops.

It would be impossible to list the many firms which produced cards throughout the war. The Inter-Art Company issued attractive coloured art work of patriotic and sentimental subjects; Arthur Butcher was one of their artists. Christensen and Piprot of France produced some attractive sentimental cards depicting the poilu usually with his girl. Though not brightly coloured they have a delicacy of design that is typically French.

War-time humour produced a spate of amusing cards, good artists and, in some cases, a high standard of production. Tom Browne was a well known and humourous artist who was employed by Davidson Bros. Series for which he was res-

ponsible included 'Soldiers of the King' and 'With the Territorials'. One of the most famous artists of war-time humour was Bruce Bairns-father. He drew for the Bystander and his work was published in book form as well as appearing on cards. His famous character, Old Bill, grew out of his own experiences for he went to France with the B.E.F. in 1914 and knew what trench warfare was like.

Among sentimental cards those issued by Bamforth were very popular depicting the Tommy's longing for home. The Inter-Art Company's Dear Heart series pursued the same theme.

Prices
As we have noted above, cards are still relatively cheap and it is only the rarities which will cost over £1 a piece. The cards which German

RETRAITE DES ALLEMANDS
Guerre 1914-15-16 17... Canon Allemand
détruit dans son abri

GERMAN RETREAT
War 1914-15-16-17... German gun destroyed
in its shelter

67m. Série

Visé, Paris No 1651

Plate 23 Postcards produced in France showing war damage and scenes of troop movements.

Guerre 1914-15   ALBERT (Somme) — Passage d'un train de Soldats Français en gare d'Albert en Août 1914
78.   A train of French Soldiers passing through the station of Albert in August 1914

Lefune, 21, rue Saint-Martin, Ainiers

prisoners of World War I in Alexandra Palace used to write home on may fetch this price, aerial cards are collectors' pieces; those which date from the early years of the century, cards representing zeppelins, airships and World War I dogfights may cost from 50p to £1 each or even higher. There are dealers who specialise in aerial material and their prices are usually high but general dealers are cheaper, particularly if cards are purchased in lots.

Boer War cards are both scarce and dear but the difficulty will be to find them. Many cards of the pre-1914 period were issued in sets and this is the way they are frequently available today. Cards purchased individually, apart from those mentioned, will probably cost from 5p to 25p each.

Each collector must decide for himself whether he prefers used or unused cards. Messages have a personal element about them which makes them attractive. The messages are often a reflection of the sentiments and attitudes of their time, often they show how little difference the passage of time or circumstance makes to basic human reactions to conditions of war. Used cards frequently bear Field Post Office frankings which increase their interest and value to collectors. For the collector not particularly concerned with frankings these may often pay for the other items in a collection; an album recently bought for £5 for 400 cards contained 20 with Field Post Office marks from France and Italy which recovered the full price paid for the album and a little more besides.

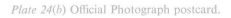

Plate 24(a) 'Daily Mail' War Picture postcard.

Plate 24(b) Official Photograph postcard.

Plate 25 Humorous cards by Tom Browne.

Books

Book collecting is a long established hobby with very distinct guide lines which apply to the ways which one may set about it. Condition is as important as in any branch of collecting and rarity is equally esteemed. The collector also expects his items to be good examples of their kind, possessing beauty and exhibiting the skills of their makers as well as their writers. To get all these things means being prepared to spend both time and money on their acquisition. The military enthusiast may also be a book collector, in which case he must certainly be prepared to pay prices for his acquisition which may well exceed the sort of maximum that we have in mind in these pages. The collector of military books would certainly not think of his collection as in any sense ephemeral. The sort of books with which we are concerned here are not, therefore, quite collector's items for the bibliophile but they do not for that reason lack interest.

In the first place the collector of militaria of any sort needs tools, books which will give him information as well as pleasure. There are a number of campaign histories which it is very useful to possess and which are not as yet too expensive, such as Nolan's *History of the Russian War*, Cassell's *History of the War between France and Germany*, Creswick's *South Africa and the Transvaal War*, Playfair and Molony's *History of the Second World War* and one or other of the still easily available histories of the First World War.

Apart from histories of campaigns, which will help to place letters, documents, regimental markings on covers and cards and other identifiable ephemera in their right context, it will be found very useful to have some reference material about some of the main categories of ephemera. For example Toni and Valmai Holt have given us a most useful guide to postcards in their *Picture Postcard of the Golden Age*, with a chapter devoted to cards of military interest; there are books on Militaria and collecting, of which that by Frederick Wilkinson is useful; among older books Hayden's *Chats on Old Prints* and Neville's *British Military Prints* are worth borrowing from the local library. The literature of Postal History, including military postal history, is less well served in books that are easily available, but the library of the Forces Postal History Society is available to members, and no collector of military ephemera will want to miss membership of this useful society. Among useful volumes are P. E. Raynor's *A Reference List of British Army Postmarks used in the Great War 1914–1919*, Col. G. Crouch and Norman Hill *British Army Post Offices 1939–1950*, K. Tranmer *Austro-Hungarian Military Post 1914–1918*.

An interesting type of book to collect, if the searcher is lucky, is the association item such as that illustrated on *Plate 26*. No one supposes these are easy to find but a search in the bookshops of garrison towns or such places to which military men retire may reveal signed or annotated copies of books which have been discarded when retirement has demanded a move to smaller accommodation. Every signature, bookplate, inscription or annotation is worth examining, checking the author with *Army List* or Regimental History.

More consistent with our definition of ephemera is the wide range of informational or propaganda material that issues from a condition of war. Official proclamations, laws national and local, have appeared at all times of national distress. The Commonwealth under Cromwell published pamphlets with Parliamentary authority for the administration of local and national affairs.

Plate 26 Fragments from France. By Captain Bruce Bairnsfather.

Though not specifically of a military nature they were the result of Civil War; among the best known was *The Directory for the Public Worship of God* and the *Ordnance of the Lords and Commons* which enforced it. It marked, in 1646, the victory of the Puritan army over the Royalist Anglicans. The French Revolution likewise was faced with the task of producing a new administrative system thoughout the nation and this produced broadsides and proclamations on military and civil matters. The two great wars of the twentieth century produced a spate of special publications for the guidance of the civil population and the raising of morale and informing those at home about the life and activities of the men on active service. Propaganda was a large part of these publications and inevitably enemy atrocities were referred to and often vividly illustrated. This is a large and interesting body of literature worthy of closer attention than it has so far received, reflecting the life and mind of people at war.

The official publications of the War Department relating to the Armed Forces themselves are a different group entirely and will be of great interest to the historian of weaponry, drill and uniform. These occasionally appear on the market but were not generally available to the public and are therefore more difficult to obtain than those such as we have illustrated.

Prices

Pamphlets of the seventeenth and eighteenth centuries will cost between £3 and £10 according to rarity, English items tending to be rather higher priced than Continental. The nineteenth century is rather cheaper and pamphlets are around £3 to £5 an item; proclamations and broadsides relatively less as the century advances. The literature of the two world wars is at present both plentiful and cheap, some items rating only a few pence and to be found in the junk boxes of booksellers.

General military histories vary according to the quality and scarcity of the publication. Nolan's *History of the Russian War* was originally issued in parts and may be found in eight volumes or two volumes, in either case costing about £7.50. Cassell's histories cost around £5 and Boer War histories a little more; there are many useful Regimental histories currently available and a wealth of publications on both world wars of the twentieth century. The shelves of the local library are the best place for finding out about these.

THE original of this Picture was painted from a Description and Plan given me by COLONEL JACKSON about the year 1874. He being an excellent Artist as well as Engineer, his help was most valuable.

He said at 2 o'clock in the morning of the 19th of June, 1815, he rode on to the field of Waterloo with the French in order to send on our troops and allies after the French on the road to Nivelles,—as already stated in the preface to his book, where he describes the picture. He was directed to translate this order into the different languages,—German and Dutch,—he being a good linguist. He said he was the only visible moving object on that vast field of death, the Sun just rising all in shade. On the extreme right the ruins of La Haie Sainte with the port holes made in haste to defend that part; a vast number of dead lay around those walls. Hougomont in mid distance. In front of the Picture, the sand pit, into which many a poor fellow fell. The next to the left was one of those erected over some Officer of rank—such as his chief, Sir William Delancey, who was mortally wounded; they were formed of 7 Muskets 3 at each end crossing each other, and one across at top, a blanket thrown over. The French cannon he observed also on the left, tumbled together in a gully with tumbrils; a confused mass. The far off object in the French lines had caused much curiosity and speculation all day among the Duke's Staff, and many glasses were directed to it; it was found afterwards to be a scaffold for engineering purposes. The rising ground seen beyond La Haie Sainte is where Colonel Jackson told me he saw the last charge of the English in full pursuit of the French, when he returned from trying to persuade the Prussian Forces to hurry up, as described in his book. Wellington and his Staff rode all day on the rising ground, on this side of the Sand Pit. The French army on the opposite hill as described before.

ANN DE LA TOUR.

NOTES AND REMINISCENCES

OF A

STAFF OFFICER,

CHIEFLY RELATING TO

THE WATERLOO CAMPAIGN,

AND TO

ST. HELENA MATTERS

DURING THE CAPTIVITY OF NAPOLEON.

BY

LIEUTENANT-COLONEL BASIL JACKSON.

PRINTED FOR PRIVATE CIRCULATION.

LONDON:
HARRISON AND SONS, ST. MARTIN'S LANE,
Printers in Ordinary to Her Majesty.
1877.

Plate 28 (a) A Voice from Waterloo by Sergeant Major E. Cotton. 1849.
Another of Lieutenant-Colonel Jackson's books.

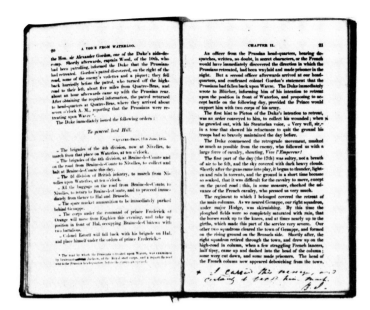

Plate 28 (b) Diary of a V.A.D. nurse

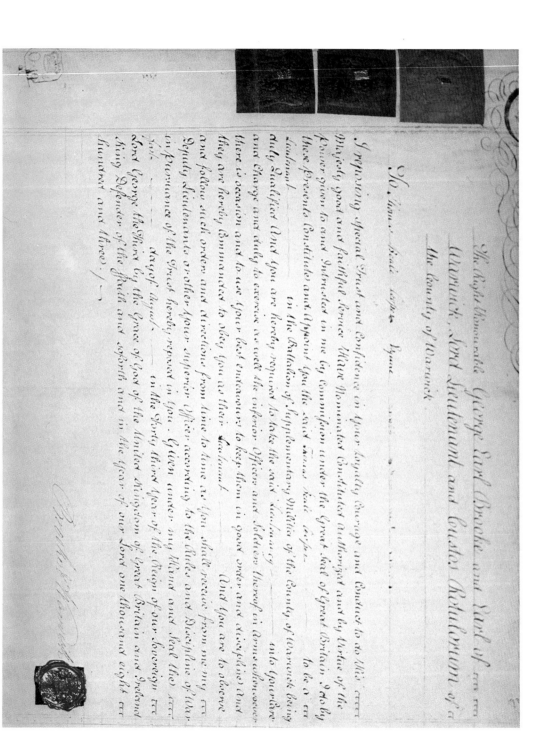

Plate 29 Commissions granted to Thomas Beale Cooper.

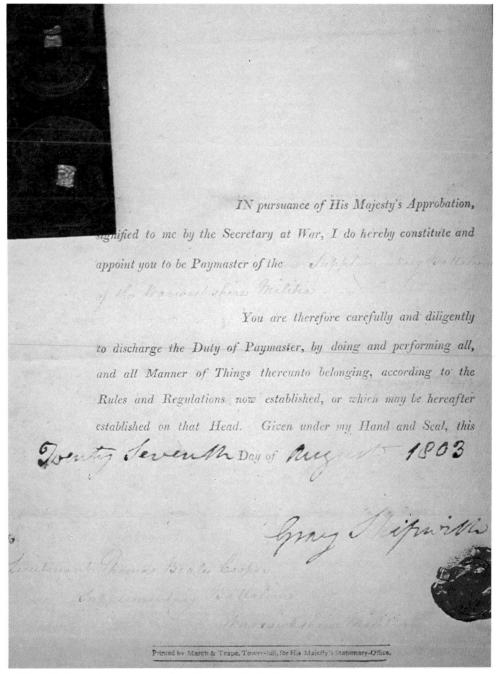

IN pursuance of His Majesty's Approbation, signified to me by the Secretary at War, I do hereby constitute and appoint you to be Paymaster of the *Supplementary Battalion of the Warwickshire Militia* —

You are therefore carefully and diligently to discharge the Duty of Paymaster, by doing and performing all, and all Manner of Things thereunto belonging, according to the Rules and Regulations now established, or which may be hereafter established on that Head. Given under my Hand and Seal, this *Twenty Seventh* Day of *August* 1803

Printed by March & Teape, Tower-hill, for His Majesty's Stationary-Office.

Plate 30 Commissions granted to Thomas Beale Cooper.

GⱯ R1

HE whom this scroll commemorates was numbered among those who, at the call of King and Country, left all that was dear to them, endured hardness, faced danger, and finally passed out of the sight of men by the path of duty and self-sacrifice, giving up their own lives that others might live in freedom.

Let those who come after see to it that his name be not forgotten.

Mr. Norman Willis Taylor
Midshipman R.N.

Plate 31 Memorial scroll for a Midshipman killed in the First World War.

Letters, Diaries, Personal Documents and Photographs

The personal nature of this class of material puts it very much at risk every time a family suffers a bereavement or even moves house. Few families can afford to accumulate the records of past members and many feel conscientiously that records of a personal sort should be destroyed when a man or woman dies.

However, they are to be found and appear in dealers' catalogues. Dates are a first guide to their likely interest. Correspondence during war-time seldom failed to mention some of the features of life to which war gave rise. This is more frequently the case in recent times when civilian populations have been so intensely affected by war conditions.

But from the letters illustrated here it is clear that comment is not confined to twentieth-century writers. The French Revolution affected the whole country and so did the bogey of Napoleon a little later when England thought itself under threat of invasion.

Personal letters from husbands at the front frequently describe conditions of life and friend-ships made under the grim conditions of battle which shed much light on human reactions to war and military service. Diaries too, are sometimes very personal documents and at other times, as with that shown here, a fascinating record of one small part of the total military operation. Diaries

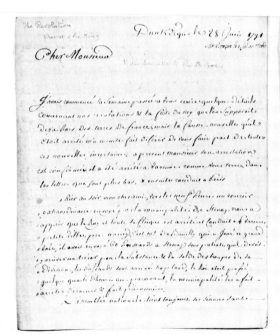

Plate 32(a) A letter from France dated June 28th 1791.

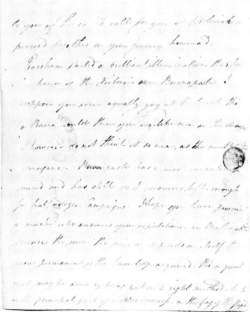

Plate 32(b) A contemporary letter describing celebrations at Evesham on the victory of the allies at Leipzig in October 1813.

and commonplace books were more frequently kept in the nineteenth than in the twentieth century and dealers frequently advertise material from the Crimea, Indian campaigns and the Boer War. These command a fair price according to length and content but are usually available from about £10 upwards. A commonplace book in the author's possession, put together by an officer of the Royal Engineers serving in India in the late-nineteenth century, cost under £2. Though containing no specific campaign material it reveals the manifold interests of an army man abroad, from the origin of Indian languages and customs to the latest methods of road and bridge building and gunnery; many newspaper cuttings are included from papers issued in India as well as at home.

Personal documents include commissions and appointments, pay books and enlistment and discharge certificates, but will exclude documents normally retained by the War Office or Unit H.Q. The Militia appointments of the eighteenth and nineteenth centuries were on vellum and tax-stamped. They are fairly imposing documents and hence tend to survive. Paybooks of pre-1914 date are not easy to find, but are in demand by medal collectors as they record medals awarded and together with the award make an attractive item. Pay books of the last war should still be available from private sources. They do not give as much information as earlier pay books which recorded the movements of an enlisted man and his clothing issue. A search of dealers' catalogues

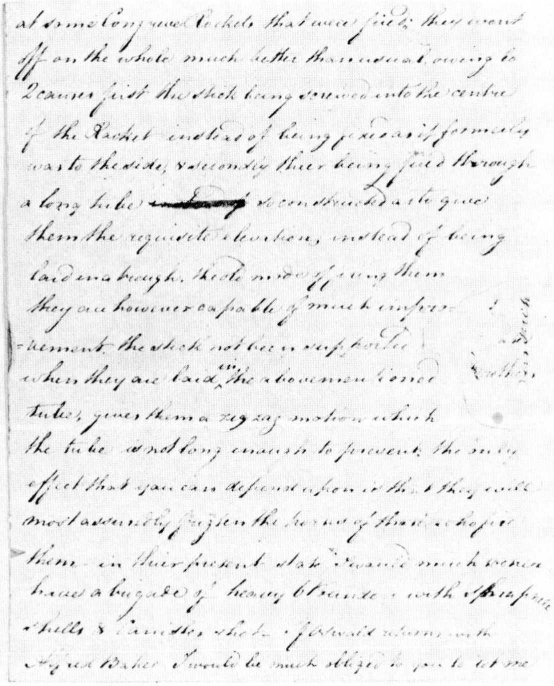

Plate 33(a) Uniform list for a cadet in the Royal Regiment of Artillery at Woolwich who completed his course of training in 1816.

Plate 33(b) A letter of 1816 from the above-mentioned officer describing an exercise with Congreve rockets.

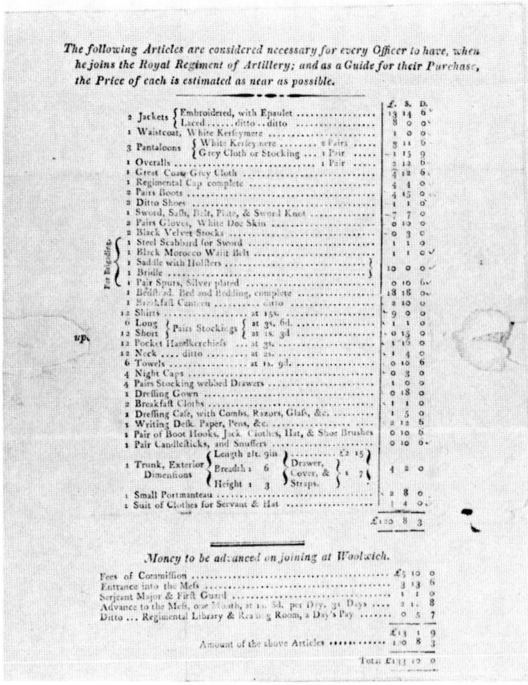

Plate 34 Appointment to a Lieutenancy in the Warwickshire militia.

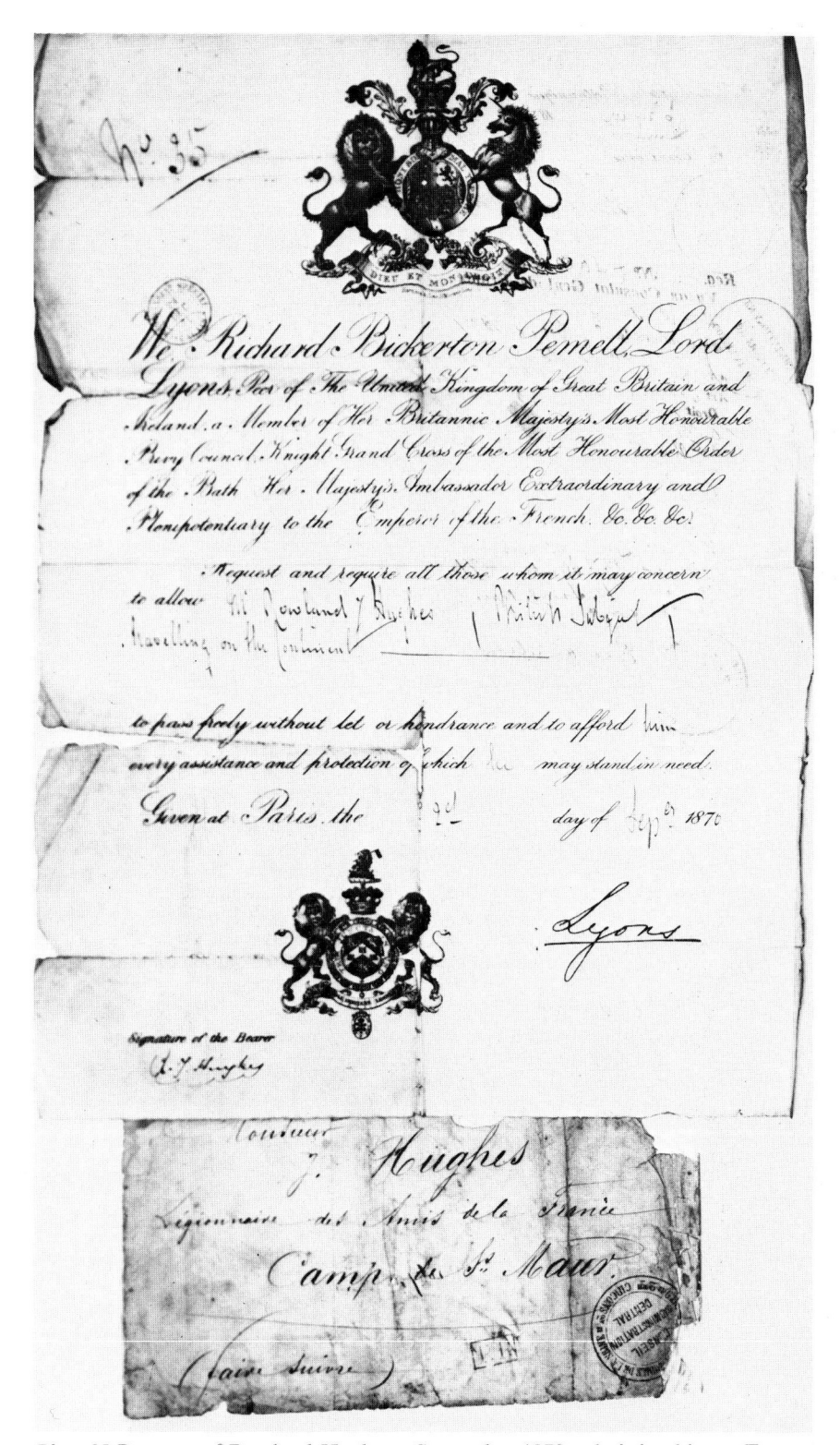

Plate 35 Passport of Rowland Hughes - September 1870, admitting him to France.

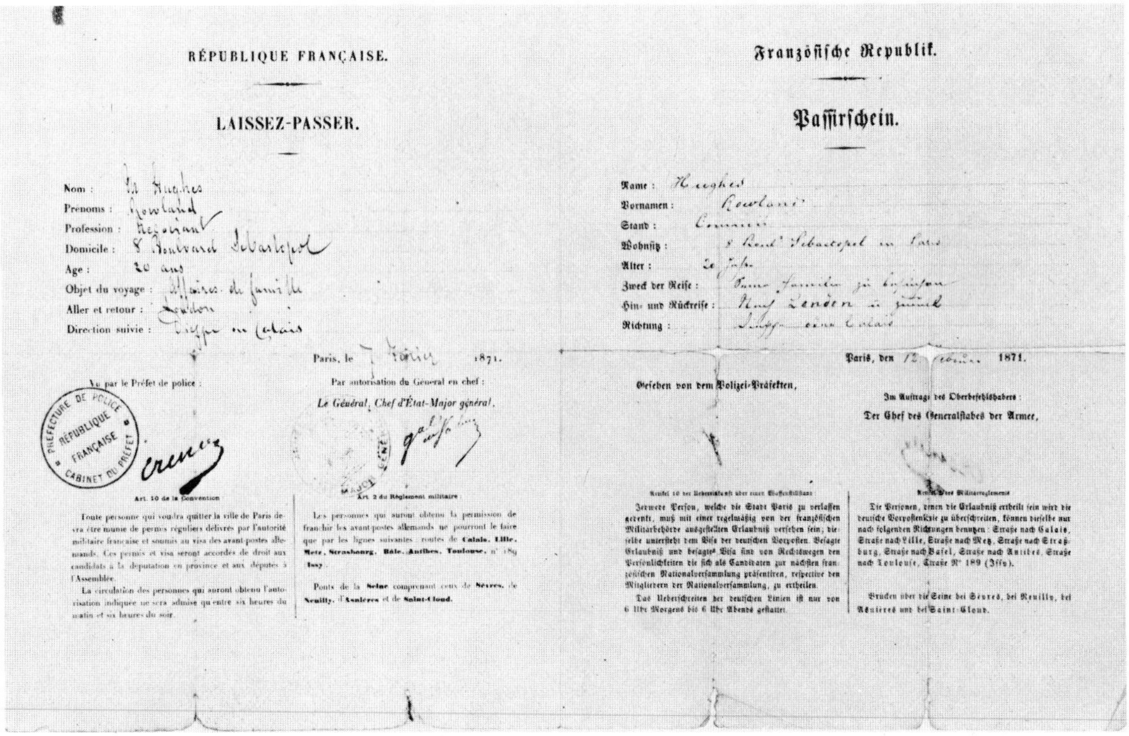

RÉPUBLIQUE FRANÇAISE.

LAISSEZ-PASSER.

Nom : Hughes
Prénoms : Rowland
Profession : Négociant
Domicile : 8 Boulevard Sébastopol
Age : 20 ans
Objet du voyage : Affaires de famille
Aller et retour : London
Direction suivie : Dieppe ou Calais

Paris, le 7 Février 1871.

Vu par le Préfet de police :

PRÉFECTURE DE POLICE · RÉPUBLIQUE FRANÇAISE · CABINET DU PRÉFET

Par autorisation du Général en chef :
Le Général, Chef d'État-Major général,

Art. 10 de la Convention

Toute personne qui voudra quitter la ville de Paris devra être munie de permis réguliers délivrés par l'autorité militaire française et soumis au visa des avant-postes allemands. Ces permis et visa seront accordés de droit aux candidats à la députation en province et aux députés à l'Assemblée.

La circulation des personnes qui auront obtenu l'autorisation indiquée ne sera admise qu'entre six heures du matin et six heures du soir.

Art. 2 du Règlement militaire

Les personnes qui auront obtenu la permission de franchir les avant-postes allemands ne pourront le faire que par les lignes suivantes : routes de **Calais**, **Lille**, **Metz**, **Strasbourg**, **Bâle**, **Antibes**, **Toulouse**, n° 189 (**Issy**).

Ponts de la **Seine** comprenant ceux de **Sèvres**, de **Neuilly**, d'**Asnières** et de **Saint-Cloud**.

Französische Republik.

Passirschein.

Name : Hughes
Vornamen : Rowland
Stand :
Wohnsitz : 8 Boul. Sebastopol in Paris
Alter : 20 Jahr
Zweck der Reise :
Hin- und Rückreise :
Richtung :

Paris, den 12 ... 1871.

Gesehen von dem Polizei-Präfekten,

Im Auftrage des Oberbefehlshabers :
Der Chef des Generalstabes der Armee,

Artikel 10 der Uebereinkunft über einen Waffenstillstand :

Jedwede Person, welche die Stadt Paris zu verlassen gedenkt, muß mit einer regelmäßig von der französischen Militärbehörde ausgestellten Erlaubniß versehen sein; dieselbe untersteht dem Visa der deutschen Vorposten. Besagte Erlaubniß und besagtes Visa sind von Rechtswegen den Persönlichkeiten die sich als Candidaten zur nächsten französischen Nationalversammlung präsentiren, respective den Mitgliedern der Nationalversammlung, zu ertheilen.

Das Ueberschreiten der deutschen Linien ist nur von 6 Uhr Morgens bis 6 Uhr Abends gestattet.

Artikel 2 des Militärreglements

Die Personen, denen die Erlaubniß ertheilt sein wird die deutsche Vorpostenlinie zu überschreiten, können dieselbe nur nach folgenden Richtungen benutzen : Straße nach Calais, Straße nach Lille, Straße nach Metz, Straße nach Straßburg, Straße nach Basel, Straße nach Antibes, Straße nach Toulouse, Straße Nr 189 (Issy).

Brücken über die Seine bei Sèvres, bei Neuilly, bei Asnières und bei Saint-Cloud.

Plate 36 Laissez-Passer with which Hughes left Paris in February 1871.

reveals very few such items and the personal approach is probably the most productive.

Photographs are increasingly scarce. Early collotypes of the 1840's and 1850's are collected for their photographic as well as their subject interest. The earliest war photographs were probably those of the Second Burma War of 1852–53. The Photographic Library of the Imperial War Museum at Lambeth has a vast collection of photographs of military interest extending from 1847 to 1914. Towards the end of the century photographic journalism reached heights of popularity in publications such as the *Illustrated London News*, the *Navy and Army Illustrated* and the *Black and White Budget*. These magazines frequently ran competitions for amateurs. Albums of personal photographs of military interest frequently come to dealers and turn up at auctions. Studio photographs of high quality frequently appear in family albums showing individuals in uniform, and groups, sometimes on enlistment or before going abroad. Amateur photographs show camp scenes, mess groups, workshops, quarters, parades. Often these are badly faded. Much can be done with modern contrast film to restore the tones by making a new black and white copy. So do not discard the faded sepia print, give it to an expert. Look carefully at named groups for names subsequently famous. For an example of the type of photograph really worth searching for look at *The Army in India, a Photographic Record 1850–1914* published in 1968 in association with the National Army Museum.

Plate 37 The Black and White Budget.

President of the British Red Cross Society

Grand Prior of the Order of St. John of Jerusalem in England

Presented by the Joint Committee of the British Red Cross Society and the Order of St. John of Jerusalem in England to Miss Vera Dagmar Bates. in recognition of valuable services rendered during the War.

Countersigned J. C. Davis Secretary

Chairman

Evelyn Cecil. Vice Chairman

1914 – 1919.

83, Pall Mall, London.

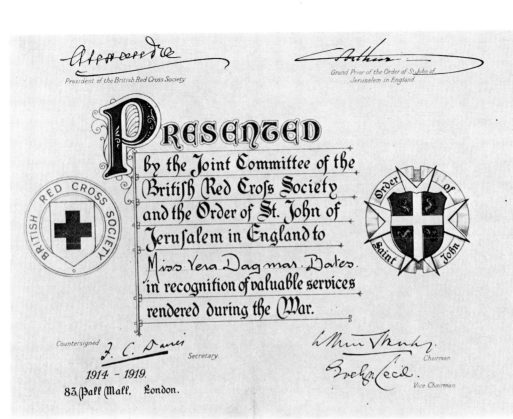

Plate 38 Red Cross and St. John's award presented to a nursing sister 1919.

Army Form W. 3022 (Part II.)

From the Regimental Paymaster or Secretary, Territorial Force Association

To Mrs G. F. Denney.

Please note that the Book of Army Allowance Forms issued in your favour for a weekly payment of 19/6 in respect of 763819 (Regl. No.) Pte O. L. Denney. (Rank) (Name) 28th County of London Battalion (Regiment)

* has been withdrawn ~~will be withdrawn~~

as payment is to cease for the following reason:—

[Reason for cessation of payment to be stated here.]

As your husband was discharged to a Commission 9-9-17; therefore will you please return your ring paper to this office immediately

Date 17-9-17 Signature

* Delete words inapplicable.

Army Form Z. 3.

IF FOUND, please drop this Certificate in a Post Office letter box.

Notice.—"This document is Government property. It is no security whatever for debt, and any person being in possession of it either as a pledge or security for debt or without lawful authority or excuse is liable under section 156 (9) of the Army Act to a fine of twenty pounds (£20) or imprisonment for six months, or to both fine and imprisonment."

PROTECTION CERTIFICATE (Officer).

The undermentioned Officer of the *Temporary Officers will be *Gazetted out of the Service. Service Category V.

with effect from 10/2/20 unless he hears to the contrary from the War Office, on and after which date he will not be entitled to draw pay. He will be entitled to wear uniform for one week from the above date and upon occasions authorized by Regulations.

Rank:— Temporary Lt

Dispersal Area No. 4B

Theatre of War or Command

Born in the year 1885

Medical Category V

Married or Single Married

Surname DENNEY

Date Stamp of Dispersal Unit or Disembarkation Office. DISPERSAL UNIT 10 FEB 1920 PURFLEET

(Signed) Rank. Commanding Commandant, No. 1 Dispersal Unit, Purfleet.

Date 9/2/20

No 126767 D/6

DEMOBILIZATION RATION BOOK.

Soldier, Sailor, or Airman.

IF FOUND, RETURN TO ANY FOOD OFFICE.

THIS BOOK IS VALID FOR A FORTNIGHT FROM THE ABOVE DATE.

N. 9x.

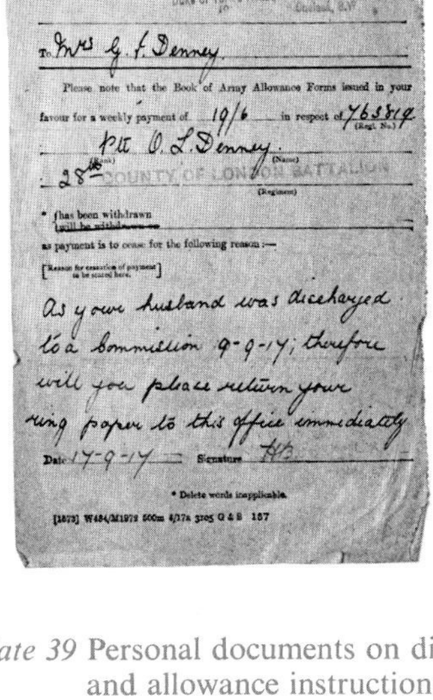

Plate 39 Personal documents on discharge 1920 and allowance instructions for the wife of a newly commissioned officer.

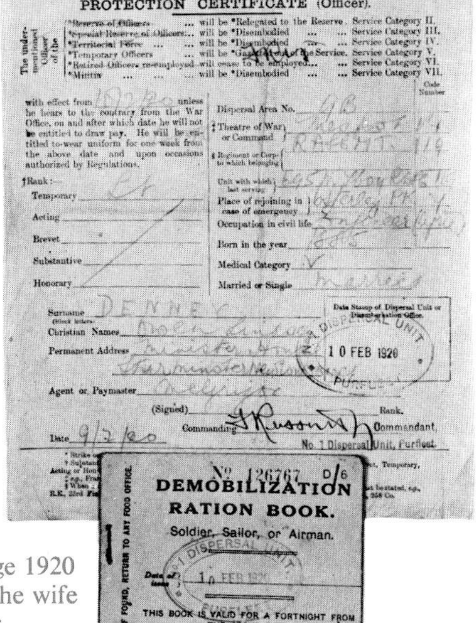

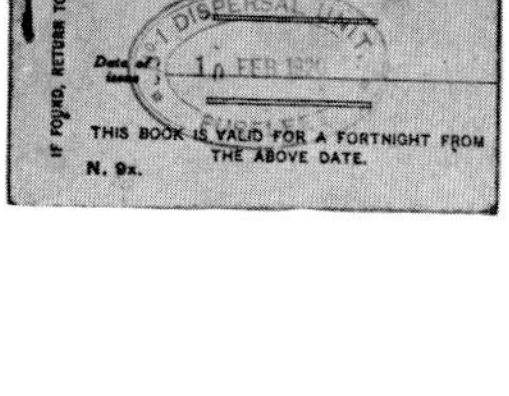

Plate 40(a) Pay Book and Release Book 1939–45.

Plate 40(b) Uniform list from military tailor 1917.

Hon. Oliver Montagu   John Brocklehurst
        Major   Captain

Alfred Egerton   F. Strickland-Constable   Sir John Willoughby, Bart.   Lord Arthur Somerset   Alexander Gordon
   Major   Lieutenant   Lieutenant   Major   Lieutenant

Hon. Lionel Byng   R. Weir   David Milne-Home   Fred Burnaby   Lord Kilmarnock   Evelyn Atherley   [Joe] Burnaby
   Lieutenant   Riding Master   Lieutenant-Colonel   Lieutenant-Colonel   Major   Captain   Lieutenant

The officers of the Blues, Regent's Park Barracks, 1882

Plate 41-42 Photographs from personal collections.

Plate 43(*a*) Artist Rifles *c.* 1890-95.

Plate 43(*b*) Petersfield Camp 1908.

Plate 43(*c*) 'B' Company 1913.

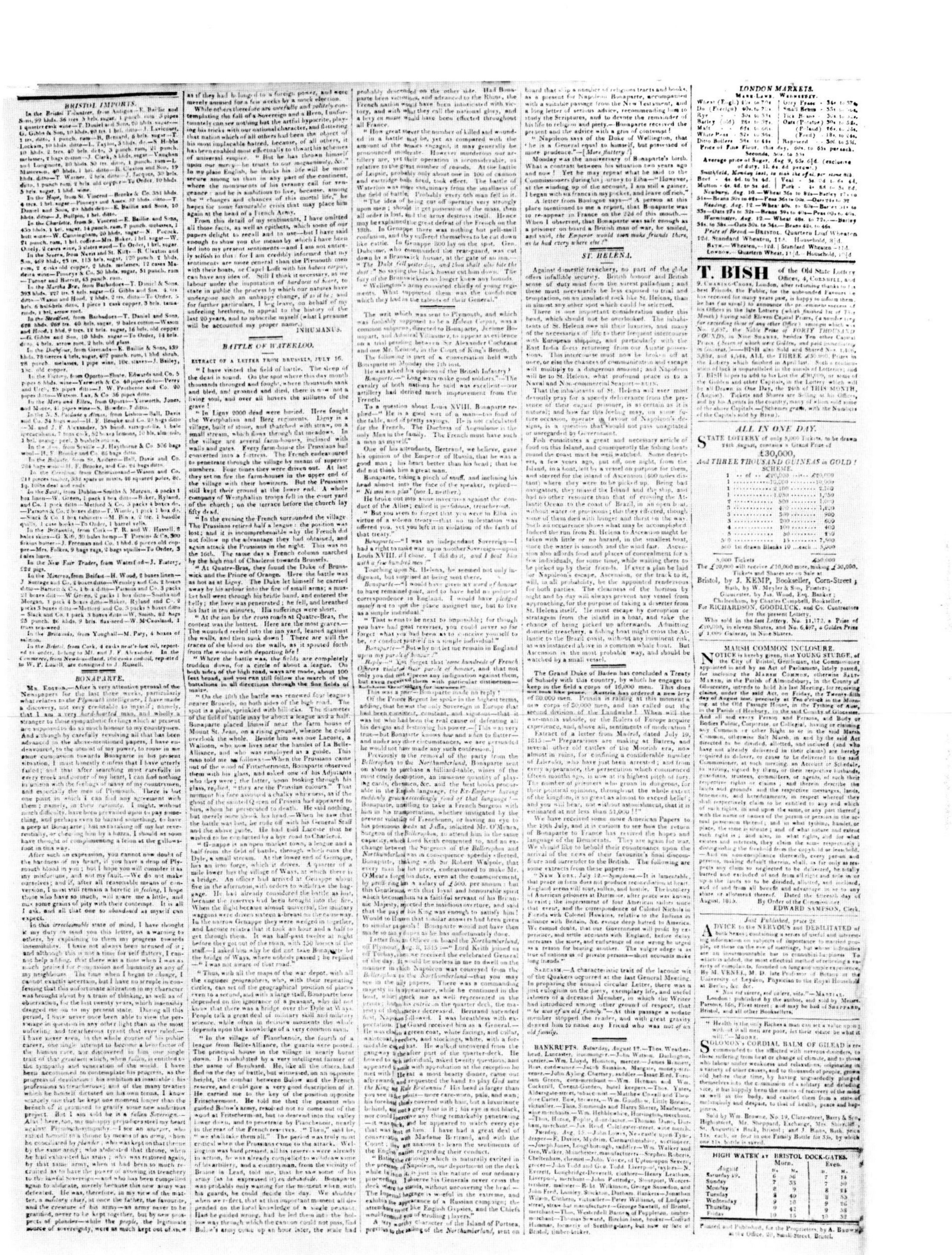
BRISTOL IMPORTS.

BONAPARTE.

BATTLE OF WATERLOO.

ST. HELENA.

LONDON MARKETS.

T. BISH

ALL IN ONE DAY.

MARSH COMMON INCLOSURE.

HIGH WATER AT BRISTOL DOCK-GATES.

Plate 44 The Bristol Mercury of August 1815.

THE RUHLEBEN CAMP MAGAZINE

No. 6.   JUNE.   **1917.**

EDITORIAL.

WE take this opportunity of thanking Sergeant Kipling, 1st. South African Infantry (an inmate of the Kriegsgefangener Lazarett, Alexandrinen Strasse, Berlin) for his highly appreciative letter of 24th January. We regret that we cannot publish his remarks in full, but thank him for the cordial spirit in which they are written, and wish him and his friends the best of luck.

THE following gentlemen duly satisfied the examiners at the London Matriculation Examination, which was held in Ruhleben in December, and we congratulate them on their success. Messrs. J. R. Hooker; C. Kemp; E. C. Macintosh; L. Nash; A. M. Pennington; L. K. White.

THE following plays have been produced in the Camp since our last number. The Marriage of Kitty. Producer, H. Goodhind; — The Tenth Man. Producer, G. Merritt; — Tantris der Narr. Producers, Leigh Henry and J. Stein; — A Pair of Spectacles. Producer, C. J. Pearce; — Das Konzert. Producer, J. Stein; — The Bells. Producer, S. Leon; — Lady Windermere's Fan. Producer, A. Welland; — Eliza comes to Stay. Producer, C. G. Pemberton; — The School for Scandal. Producer, C. Duncan Jones; — General John Regan. Producer, R. D. Carty; — La Belle Aventure. Producer, M. Perrot; — The Frogs. Producer, C. Lockyer Roberts; — Good Friday. Producer, C. Duncan Jones; — The Yeomen of the Guard. Producer, J. Corless; — The Merry Wives of Windsor. Producer, A. Welland.

AN exhibition of humorous drawings was given in the Studio in April. The drawings, which were contributed by Messrs. Wade, Walker and Wood gained the unqualified admiration of all who visited the exhibition. The thanks of the Camp are due to the artists whose genuinely funny but unobtrusive gifts have done so much to show us that there is a humorous side even to Lager life, and it affords us very much pleasure to put on record these few words of appreciation.

NEARLY seven thousand copies of the R. C. M. Christmas number were sold. Of these, four thousand and ninety three were sent to different parts of the world, including (in addition to Great Britain) Argentine 2; British Colonies 131; Chili 3; Denmark 16; Egypt 3; France 57; Holland 40; Italy 4; Japan 4; Norway 2; Persia 1; Portugal 2; Russia 4; Spain 2; Sweden 5; Switzerland 86; U. S. A. 68.

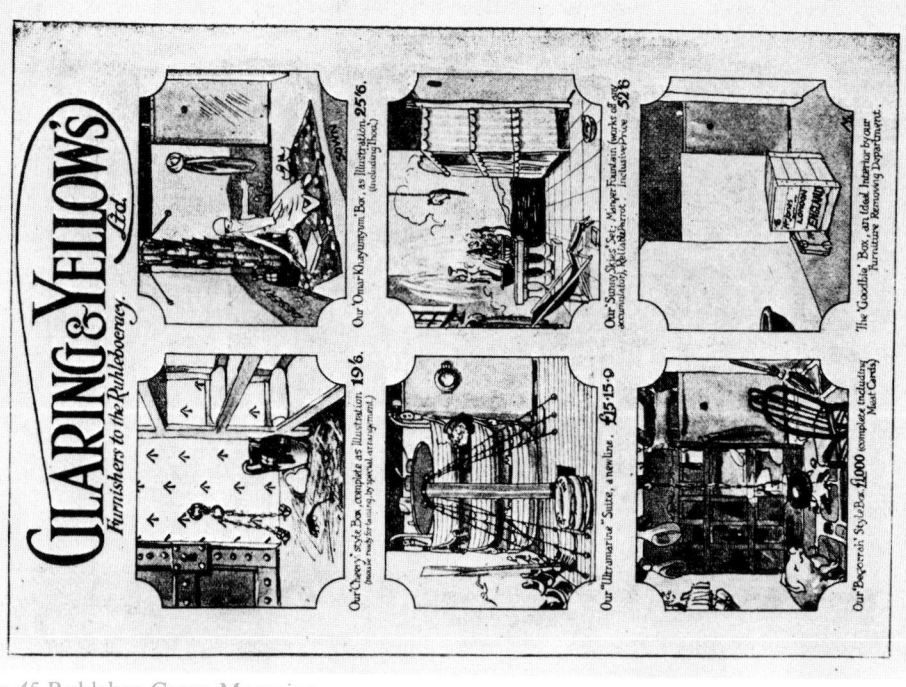

Plate 45 Ruhleben Camp Magazine.

Newspapers

The last two and a half centuries have shown remarkably little change in what constitutes news. A look at newspapers of the eighteenth century provides just the same sort of mixture of foreign intelligence with an emphasis upon matters of war and trade; scandal among the aristocracy and local 'shocking' events as we might expect in our daily papers today. The main body of the press emanated from the county towns, but often commanded a wide circulation. The *Worcester Herald* at the end of the eighteenth century reckoned to have 'an extensive circulation through the Counties of Gloucester, Hereford, Warwick, Stafford, Salop and South Wales'. The *Bristol Mercury*, judging from its advertisements, reckoned to cover most of the south-western counties and South Wales. The *Ipswich Journal* in the 1740s was sold in Bury St. Edmunds, Yarmouth, and Colchester. The *Norwich Gazette* in the 1720s covered Norfolk and included advertisements for towns in the north part of the county of Suffolk. By the turn of the century the *Ipswich Journal* had added to its title *'and Suffolk, Norfolk, Essex and Cambridgeshire Advertiser'*.

Apart from the London and the local news, the papers contain dispatches from the European capitals. Communication was slow when the horse and the boat were the only means of travel but it is quite surprising how rapidly news travelled. The *Norwich Gazette* on Thursday December 21st 1727 reported from Holland news received the previous Tuesday. This recorded events of December 4th in Madrid; on January 8th 1728 was reported news from Petersburg of December 20th and of Venice of December 30th. On January 20th was reported Paris news of January 16th and London news of January 18th. The *Bristol Mercury* almost a hundreds years later was not

doing any better, on July 30th 1813 it was reporting 'Paris Journals to the 26th instant last night reached town'. On August 2nd the *Mercury* carried the following news: 'London, Wednesday July 28th. 'The dispatches from Lieut.-Gen.Sir George Prevost, of which the substance was given in a Bulletin on Saturday, were published Sunday in an Extraordinary Gazette. – The first dispatch dated Kingston, Upper Canada, May 18th gives Major Gen. Sir R. Sheaff's account of the capture of Fort York by the Americans, on April 27th.' There follow more details of later dispatches to June 14th with lists of killed and wounded.

Since wars and rumours of wars were an almost constant state of affairs somewhere on the continent of Europe throughout the eighteenth and nineteenth centuries military information is obtainable from almost any issue of a newspaper. But as the nineteenth century advanced home affairs and political party polemic took up more and more space and papers such as the *Examiner* emerged with little space to give to foreign affairs.

Papers of this earlier period were mostly weeklies and consisted of only four pages. They were not therefore, as bulky and unmanageable as the modern press. They were frequently bound up into volumes of two or three years and took their place on the library shelves of country houses. In this way they are to be found in the bookshops or auction rooms where complete libraries are bought and sold. They are, of course, of great interest to the local historian and may, therefore, command relatively high prices. The nineteenth-century newspapers are larger in format and in number of pages and present problems of storage since it is difficult to store them satisfactorily without folding.

Some problems arise with the collection of modern papers. They are numerous, quite easily obtainable and bulky. Shall the complete paper be kept or are cuttings with special reference to other parts of the collection preferable? Newspaper cuttings have, for many people, replaced the commonplace book of the last century, and are of interest if a collection of cuttings on a single topic and covering a fair period of time can be found. The *Diary* of a V.A.D. nurse illustrated on page 41 is filled out with a number of cuttings which together give a vivid picture of the background to the events recorded in the *Diary*. They would take a very long search to compile from newspapers that the collector might hope to find

on the market. Cuttings relating to the careers of individual soldiers are also of great interest. However, copies of the dailies in which major events are recorded are certainly worth adding to a collection. Their interest is confirmed by the present reprints which are appearing on newsagents' stalls. The whole copy is worth preserving because it reflects the total interests and concerns of the moment. The copy of *Independance Belge* illustrated below is of interest in itself as the journal of an occupied country operating first as an underground publication produced in Belgium and later transferring to London for the benefit of

Plate 46 Belgian newspaper - Independance Belge.

The Prime Minister made the following announcement to-day:—

The Armistice was signed at Five o'clock this morning, and hostilities are to cease on all Fronts at 11 a.m. to-day.

FOCH CALLS THE "HALT!"

TROOPS NOT TO PASS BEYOND LINE REACHED AT 11.

"CEASE FIRE" ON ALL FRONTS.

EVACUATION BY ENEMY EXTENDED TO 31 DAYS.

The following messages were issued to-day through the wireless stations of the French Government:—

Hostilities will cease on the whole front as from November 11 at 11 o'clock (French time).

The Allied troops will not until a further order go beyond a line reached on that date and at that hour.

(Signed) MARSHAL FOCH.

PEACE!

FATE OF THE FUGITIVE KAISER.

Plate 47 Evening News for Armistice Day 1918.

the Belgian refugees in Great Britain. The personal column in which refugees seek information about one another reflects in a poignant way the personal tragedies and family break-ups that were the result of the exodus from Belgium to Britain.

Along with newspapers, the collector will frequently come across the weekly magazines which were illustrated with art work and photography. The *Illustrated London News* employed some of the best artists of the time to depict important items of news before photo-journalism took over.

Attention has been drawn to these under 'Prints' but they are also useful for their news and feature articles as well as their illustrations. Military magazines are always informative and reliable. Of particular interest are magazines produced in P.O.W. camps as the Ruhleben Camp Magazine from which the illustration on page 56 is taken. This copy runs to 72 pages of drawings, cartoons, poems and articles which give a vivid picture of how P.O.W's passed their time.

Nr. 137, Donnerstag, 31. August 1944

NACHRICHTEN FÜR DIE TRUPPE

Die Alliierten sind bereits 140 km von Saarbrücken

Reims und Rouen gefallen

Amerikanische Panzer sind über Reims hinaus und vor St. Quentin auf breiter Front im Vormarsch auf die belgische Grenze.

Gleichzeitig haben englische Panzer die Stadt Beauvais, mehr als 50 km ostwärts der unteren Seine, genommen und stossen in Richtung Amiens gegen die Somme vor.

Von der Kanalküste bis in den Raum ostwärts Reims besteht jetzt keine zusammenhängende Abwehrfront mehr.

Ostwärts Reims, das gestern von den deutschen Truppen geräumt wurde, haben alliierte Panzerspitzen bereits den Ardennen-Kanal erreicht. Vor St. Quentin haben die Amerikaner die Aisne weit hinter sich gelassen und werden um Stadtrand von Laon entfernt, 60 km von der belgischen Grenze.

Die alliierte Umfassungsbewegung quer durch Nordost-Frankreich, die alle deutschen Truppen zwischen der Seine-Mündung und der Somme abzuschneiden droht, hat bereits drei der fünf Hauptstrassen durchschnitten, auf denen die Überreste der deutschen 7. und 15. Armee sich nach Osten absetzen, um die Reichsgrenze zu erreichen.

Die Alliierten sind auf ihrem Vorstoss über die Marne bei St. Dizier und Joinville bis auf 140 km an Saarbrücken herangekommen. Deutsche Widerstandsnester an der aufgegebenen Marne-Linie liegen bereits weit hinter der Kampffront.

Auf Belgien zu

Auf ihrem Vormarsch von der Aisne zur Oise stossen die Alliierten fast nirgends auf geordneten Widerstand. Die deutschen Truppen, die in diesem Abschnitt gelegt werden sollten, werden nördlich Paris durch starke alliierte Panzer- und Infanterieverbände gefesselt.

Während die Alliierten auf breiter Front gegen die belgische Grenze vorstossen, schlagen die französischen Maquis jetzt auch in Nordost-Frankreich los.

Die deutschen Besatzungen und Stützpunkte werden überall im Rücken angegriffen, Strassen eröffnen das Feuer auf die deutschen Truppen noch bevor der Verteidigung einer Stadt vorbereitet werden kann. Während die Strassenkämpfe im Gange sind, kommen die Panzer angerollt und stossen weiter vor. Die Besatzungstruppen werden von den Maquis in Schach gehalten.

Im Abschnitt nördlich Paris haben die Alliierten jetzt fast das gesamte Ostufer der Seine besetzt und ihre Brückenköpfe zu einer

(Fortsetzung Seite 4)

Deutsche Verluste seit der Invasion

Seit dem Beginn der Invasion in Nordfrankreich sind 403.000 deutsche Soldaten gefallen, verwundet oder in Gefangenschaft geraten. Nach Meldungen von alliierter Seite befinden sich über 200.000 Mann in Gefangenschaft.

Nicht eingerechnet sind die 45.000 Mann, die bisher in Südfrankreich als tot, verwundet oder gefangen gemeldet werden. Die Zahl der deutschen Gefangenen beträgt bisher 35.000 Mann. Verloren wurden am 6. Juni ferner 1.292 Panzer, 23.000 Fahrzeuge und 1.600 Geschütze.

geschlossenen Front verschmolzen.

Während am Westufer der Seine zwischen der Mündung und Rouen noch Überreste von vier Infanterie-Divisionen und einer Panzer-Division zurückgeblieben sind und versuchen, sich den Kampf ein. Das ganze Erdölgebiet Rumäniens ist nun in der Hand sowjetischer und rumänischer Truppen, wodurch die deutsche Wehrmacht rund 150.000 Tonnen Treibstoff pro Monat mit einem Schlag verliert.

Über Ploesti führen eine Rollbahn und die Eisenbahn über die Karpaten nach Kronstadt. Mit der Einnahme von Ploesti haben die Sowjets eine neue Einfallstrasse nach Siebenbürgen und Ungarn gewonnen.

40 km von Dieppe

Von Rouen, das gestern von den deutschen Truppen geräumt werden musste, stossen alliierte Panzer und schnelle Truppen parallel zur Kanalküste nach Osten vor und haben Le Havre abgeschnitten.

Vorausabteilungen werden hier bereits 40 km südlich Dieppe gemeldet. Weiter südlich rasen die Panzer über Beauvais und Gournay, 50 km ostwärts der Seine, in Richtung auf Amiens weiter.

Bei dem raschen Tempo des

Sowjets nehmen Ölstadt Ploesti

jetzt ist er dran

Die grosse Ölstadt Ploesti wurde gestern von den Sowjets genommen.

Die deutschen Stützpunkte, die sich bisher gegen rumänische Truppen noch gehalten hatten, wurden überrannt oder stellten den Kampf ein.

Voraussichtlich wurde gemeldet, dass Sowjet-Fallschirmspringer auch den Ghymespass besetzt haben, und über den Pass in Ungarisch-Siebenbürgen eindringen. Immer mehr Stützpunkte fallen den Sowjets für ihr weiteres Vordringen gen auf Budapest und Wien in die Hände.

Im Dobrudscha, wo die Sowjets am Dienstag den grossen Hafen Konstanza genommen haben, erreichten russische Kolonnen jetzt das bulgarische Grenzgebiet.

Auf der Donau dampfen jetzt Kanonenboote der russischen Schwarz-Meerflotte flussaufwärts und beschiessen die deutschen Stützpunkte im Raum des Donauhafens Giurgiu. Ein Stützpunkt nach dem andern wird eingekesselt und muss die Waffen strecken. Die Sowjets stehen 25 km von Bukarest.

Generale ergeben sich

Im Kessel am unteren Sereth ergaben sich am Dienstag ein kommandierender General und drei Divisionskommandeure mit dem Rest ihrer Truppen — insgesamt 15.000 Mann — den Sowjets.

Sie sind der kommandierende General des VII. A.K., General der Artillerie Ernst Hell, der Kommandeur der 79. Infanterie-Division, Generalleutnant Weinknecht, der Kommandeur der 258. Infanterie-Division, Oberst Fischer, und der Kommandeur der 106. Infanterie-Division, Oberst Rintenberg.

Im Hauptquartier von Generaloberst Friessner rechnet man damit, dass die Sowjets schon in den nächsten Tagen ganz Rumänien besetzt haben und zum konzentrischen Angriff auf Ungarn übergehen werden. Nur

(Fortsetzung Seite 4)

Gen. Feldm. Model endgültig zum OB-West ernannt

Generalfeldmarschall Model ist jetzt endgültig als neuer OB-West bestätigt worden.

Generalfeldmarschall von Kluge hatte seinen Oberbefehl im Westen nicht mehr ausgeübt seit seinem letzten Besuch im Führerhauptquartier, wohin er am 13. August nach dem Fehlschlagen der Führeroffensive bei Mortain zu einer Lagebesprechung abgereist war.

In der Umgebung des abgesetzten OB-West war seit längerem bekannt, dass Generalfeldmarschall von Kluge stärkste Einwendungen gegen die wiederholten Eingriffe des Führers in die Leitung der Operationen erhoben hatte.

Insbesondere hatte Generalfeldmarschall von Kluge starke Bedenken geäussert gegen die Führeroffensive bei Mortain, als der Führer dem Obergruppenführer Hausser Befehl gab, mit ungenügenden Kräften und ohne Fliegerunterstützung den verhängnisvollen Durchbruchsversuch in Richtung Avranches zu unternehmen.

Generalfeldmarschall von Kluge war genau 38 Tage OB-West.

Er war am 6. Juli ernannt worden zugleich von Generalfeldmarschall von Rundstedt, der genau 30 Tage nach Beginn der Invasion enthoben wurde.

Korpsgruppe Kniess kämpft um Ausweg

Im Rhonetal zwischen Montelimar und Valence versuchen die Reste der Korpsgruppe Kniess, sich den Weg nach Norden zu öffnen. Eine Pontonbrücke, die nachts über die Drome bei Livron gebaut wurde, wurde wieder unter dem Bombenhagel der Anglo-Amerikaner, ehe noch deutsche Kolonnen sie überqueren konnten.

Weiter nördlich versuchen Panzer der 11. Pz. Div. den Weg nach Valence durchzuschlagen, das von den Maquis gehalten wird.

Nach Meldungen der Alliierten haben sich von der Armeegruppe Blaskowitz bei der anglo-amerikanischen Landung in Südfrankreich bereits über 45.000 Mann ergeben. In dieser Zahl sind die Truppen nicht inbegriffen, die von französischen Freischärlern gefangen genommen wurden.

Auch Vize-Admiral Ruhfus, der Kommandeur des Marinestützpunkts Toulon und die von ihm befehligten Einheiten sind in Gefangenschaft.

Neue Ritterkreuze

Das Ritterkreuz des Eisernen Kreuzes erhielten:

Generalmajor Heinrich Kittel, Kampfkommandant von Lemberg ; Major Fritz Bader Kommandeur eines Hochgebirgs-Jäger-Bataillons ;

Unteroffizier Martin Kiefer, Gruppenführer in einem bayrischen Grenadier-Regiment.

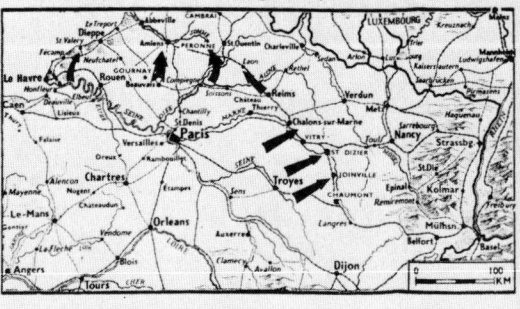

Plate 48 News Sheet dropped by the R.A.F. in advance of allied troops. August 1944.

Prints

Of all printed militaria, prints are probably the most attractive and most sought after. During the sixteenth and seventeenth centuries there were several books, both on the art and science of war and on history of warfare. Several of these are illustrated by wood engravings, not, of course, at this date in colour. Detail is therefore of little value for the history of uniform and the engravings are crude but information about tactics, drill and the handling of weapons can be gained from them. A fine example is a Dutch publication: *J. de Gheyn Wapenhandelinghe van Roers Musquetten ende Spiessen*, with 108 fine copperplates, published in Amsterdam in 1608, and Robert Ward's *Animadversions of War* published in 1639 with numerous wood engravings in the text. Such books as these are uncommon and expensive. More frequently to be found are the many beautiful publications of the eighteenth and nineteenth centuries with copper and steel engravings and, in the nineteenth century, colour plates of high quality. The introduction of chromolithography in the second quarter of the century made the coloured illustration cheaper and vastly enhanced the number and quality of colour plate books.

Francis Grose, a well known antiquarian and artist who died in 1791 after a prolific career as writer and illustrator of his own books, assembled a wealth of material for a history of the British Army. This appeared in 1801 and included plates which showed his use of de Gheyn's work. The advent of lithography under the guidance of Rudolph Ackemann at the beginning of the nineteenth century heralded a number of coloured plate books of which the *Microcosm of London* is the most famous, but which included the *Loyal Volunteers of London and its Environs* with eighty-seven plates by Rowlandson. It is interesting for the military historian to note that Acker-

mann was more than a publisher, he was an inventor and actually produced a balloon for dropping propaganda leaflets over enemy territory, but unfortunately it was never put to use.

In 1819 Edward Orme published *Historic and Military Anecdotes* with twenty aquatint plates. He is better known for his publications on Field Sports, but the end of the Napoleonic wars gave publishers a chance to record the events of these many campaigns and Orme was one who seized the opportunity of catching the interest of the public.

The imperial age opened with the numerous campaigns in which England, France, Germany, Russia and Portugal were engaged all over the world and interest in military matters increased and many books appeared on current events and regimental histories. Richard Cannon, clerk at the Horse Guards from 1802 to 1854, produced his *Historical Records of the British Army*. This work comprised a wealth of regimental history and was embellished with coloured plates to illustrate regimental uniform.

The books so far mentioned are difficult to find nowadays; the earlier ones are frequently broken up and the prints sold separately. This is unfortunate for the book lover but, like books of maps, they would be so expensive complete that few buyers would be able to afford the luxury of a Rowlandson if he had to buy twenty at a time. Even as separate prints they are likely to cost up to £50 a time.

Towards the end of the century a number of illustrators appeared whose work is of good quality and sufficiently plentiful to be obtainable by the moderate purse at about £4 to £5. Such are Richard Sinkin, Captain Oakes-Jones, Caton Woodville and others who continued to work well into the present century.

HALIFAX GARRISON ARTILLERY.

Plate 49 Halifax Garrison Artillery.

THE CAPE MOUNTED RIFLES.

Plate 50 The Cape Mounted Rifles.

SERGEANT AND PRIVATE OF THE DUBLIN FUSILIERS.

Photo by Gregory & Co., London.

Plate 51 Photographic illustration from L. Creswicke: South Africa and the Transvaal War.

Before leaving the print, attention must be drawn to the more truly ephemeral illustration. In the last half of the last century and throughout the present, magazines and newspapers have used first class artists, both draughtsmen and photographers. Among the former have been the often anonymous or little known illustrators of the pages of such publications as the *Illustrated London News*, *Boys Own Paper*, *Bystander*, *Answers* and many others which flourished before photographic journalism eclipsed the graphic illustrator.

Recently the development of methods of colour reproduction has made it possible for copies of previously unobtainable material to be purchased in reproductions which are often almost indistinguishable from the original. To add to the collector's problems these reproductions are often sold framed which makes identification even more difficult. The best way of avoiding the disappointment of being sold a reproduction is to do some preliminary self-education. Take a small magnifying glass to a museum or library where originals are available and study the texture and composition of the print and the paper and then compare them with those of a known reproduction. A little practice should enable you to detect reproduction even when framed under glass.

Plate 52 Photographic illustration from L. Creswicke: South Africa and the Transvaal War.

Plate 53 Christmas cards of World War I.

Plate 54 Cigarette Cards depicting n
uniform, head-dress, meda
regimental badges and stan

PLAYER'S CIGARETTES

COMMEMORATIVE MEDAL.
BELGIUM.

PLAYER'S CIGARETTES

MILITARY ORDER OF SAVOY.
ITALY.

WILLS'S CIGARETTES.

MAHARAJAH SIR PERTAB SINGHJI.

PLAYER'S CIGARETTES

ORDER OF EL NAHDA.
HEDJAZ.

PLAYER'S CIGARETTES.

Private, 45th Foot, 1748.

PLAYER'S CIGARETTES.

CAP BADGE.

Royal North Devon Yeomanry. (Hussars).
Now 96th (Devonshire Yeomanry) Brigade, R.F.A. (2 Battalions).

PLAYER'S CIGARETTES.

CAP BADGE.

Lothians and Border Horse Yeomanry.
Now 19th (Lothians & Border Horse) Armoured Car Coy., Tank Corps.

PLAYER'S CIGARETTES.

Officer, 17th Lt. Dragoons, 1810.

PLAYER'S CIGARETTES.

1st LIFE GUARDS:
Officer's full dress helmet, 1860.

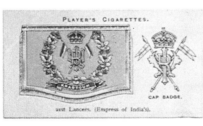

PLAYER'S CIGARETTES.

CAP BADGE.

21st Lancers. (Empress of India's).

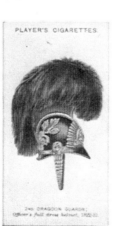

PLAYER'S CIGARETTES.

Private, Derbyshire Regiment, 1855.

PLAYER'S CIGARETTES.

Trooper,
3rd (Prince of Wales's) Dragoons, 1810.

PLAYER'S CIGARETTES.

15th THE KING'S HUSSARS:
Officer's full dress shako, 1834.

PLAYER'S CIGARETTES.

2nd DRAGOON GUARDS:
Officer's full dress helmet, 1902-20.

V.C. HEROES — BOER WAR
No 79.

Trooper Morris, V.C.
of the N.S. Wales Lancers, exhibited the
victory in China for rescuing a comrade,
whose horse was shot under him, under the
point-blank fire of Mausers.

Plate 56 Welcome Home to troops returning from South Africa, November 1900.

Plate 55 Raising a loan to buy out an officer of the Regiment in order to gain promotion.

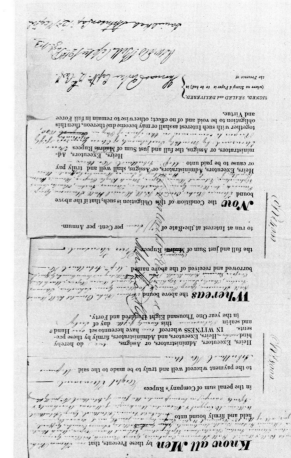

Stamps

Collecting stamps for the sake of the theme represented on them has developed into a recognised part of philately and the designers as well as the dealers are doing their part. The military theme has appeared in various forms for many years. Bulgaria has some interesting examples – a cherrywood canon used against the Turks appears on the 5st. value of 1901 commemorating the 25th anniversary of the War of Independence, the battle of Shipka Pass appears on a 1902 issue and the 1934 issue for the unveiling of Shipka Pass Memorial includes appropriate themes from the same battle. European issues associated with liberation, independence, national militarism and war abound and a choice may be made of any specific theme by reference to *Gibbons European Catalogues*. There are similar issues among the stamps of South America, China, Syria and Egypt, in fact any country which has undergone change of government by violent means has commemorated the fact on stamps.

Military uniform is in many ways a more attractive and colourful theme than war and revolution and many issues of recent years have appeared among commonwealth countries. In 1969 St. Helena issued a set of four stamps depicting the K.S.L.I. of 1815, the Lancashire Fusiliers 1816, Artilleryman 1820, and Sappers and Marines 1832. A similar set came from Gibraltar the same year and Antigua has issued sets in 1970, 1971 and 1972. Since these sets are recent they are easy to obtain and inexpensive. Aden, New Zealand and South Africa all have stamps depicting members of the armed forces in uniform. Portuguese colonial stamps have some superb period uniform sets such as those of Guinea issued in 1966 (8 stamps).

There are several dealers who specialise in thematic material and their names and addresses appear regularly in weekly and monthly journals which are available at newsagents.

Another most interesting and instructive theme with military and political history as its background is the host of over-printed stamps which appeared after the 1914–18 war to provide for the forces of occupation and the plebiscites and mandates which eventually shaped the modern map of Europe. A most stimulating series of articles by J. A. Williams appeared in the magazine *Stamp Collecting* in 1967 (April to July issues) entitled Europe after the First World War. The articles cover occupation issues as well as those which followed the peace. Such a theme gives scope for endless research and writing up and many of the stamps are becoming scarce. A similar series of articles with more emphasis on the depiction of the theme of War appeared in *Gibbons Stamp Monthly* in January, March and May of 1965, *The First World War, a Philatelic Review* by S. H. Norris. He continued the theme with the aftermath of the First World War in the issues from July to November of the same year. A good article on the stamps associated with the Russo-Turkish War appeared in the *Stamp Magazine* by J. A. Mackay in July 1968. The French Empire was very much a matter of military conquest and the leading servicemen involved appear on many of the colonial issues. S. H. Norris again supplied the philatelic background to French Imperialism in articles in the April to July 1967, October to November 1968, and January 1969 numbers of *Gibbons Stamp Monthly*. This project approach offers a long term collecting interest and the opportunity to apply specialised philatelic knowledge and research. Many overprinted stamps are forged, the Fiume overprints on Hungary and many of the mandate overprints also attracted clever forgers whose work is not always easy to

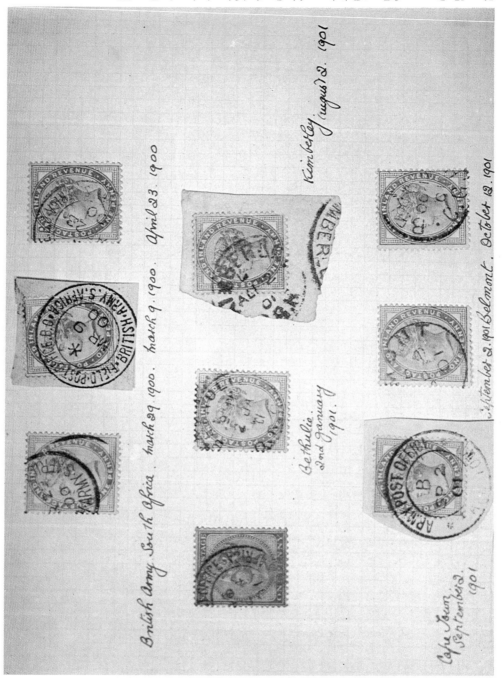

Kimberley. August 2. 1901

April 23. 1900

March 9. 1900.

Bethulie.
2nd January 1901

British Army. South Africa. March 29.1900.

September 2. 1901 Belmont. October 12. 1901

Cafe Town.
September 3.
1901

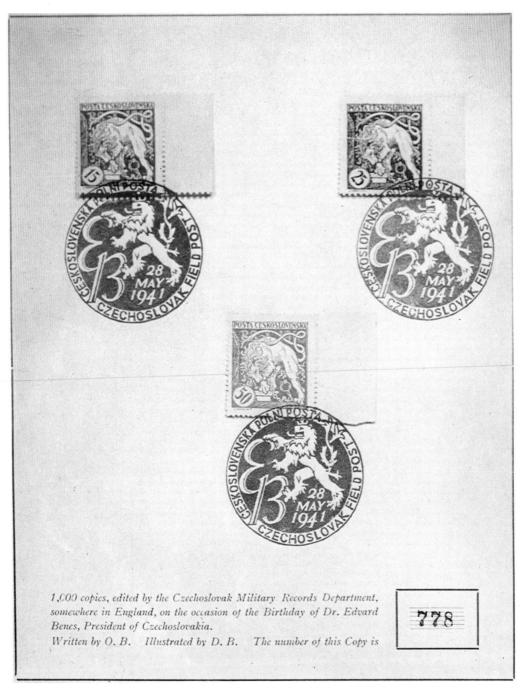

1,000 copies, edited by the Czechoslovak Military Records Department, somewhere in England, on the occasion of the Birthday of Dr. Edvard Benes, President of Czechoslovakia.
Written by O. B.   Illustrated by D. B.   The number of this Copy is

778

Plate 58 Commemorative folder to President Dr E. Benes on his 57th birthday by the Czechoslovak Army and Air Force in Great Britain, 28th May 1941.

detect. When purchasing overprinted stamps of this period do so from a reputable dealer such as Stanley Gibbons or seek the help of an expert.

Attention has been drawn to special military postmarks in the section on military postal history, but there have also been numerous issues of stamps specially for the use of servicemen. Egypt issued special seals and stamps for the use of British Forces in Egypt in 1932–35. Germany issued military fieldpost stamps from 1942 to 1944 including one depicting a Junkers 52 transport plane which was cleverly forged by the British authorities. The Austrian military post issues of 1914–18 are well known and filled the pages of many schoolboy albums of the 1920s.

Prisoner of War Camps had internal mail services organised by the prisoners who printed their own stamps. These of course were not official postage stamps and do not appear in the catalogues. They are what philatelists call 'cinderella' stamps. Ruhleben camp (see *Plate 3*) issued stamps as well as stationery. In more recent years the seamen of eight different nationalities stranded in the Great Bitter Lake as a result of the Suez troubles in 1967, issued their own stamps which have been accepted by post offices in Egypt, Switzerland, Austria and Greece when mailed by men on leave from the ships.

The Nigeria-Biafra war resulted in the issue of stamps for the short lived Republic of Biafra. A fascinating but difficult field for the collector is the period before the establishment of the People's Republic of China. Stamps were issued for various regions and uses and there are very many overprints and special use issues, including military post.

From these few remarks it can be seen what a great variety of theme and interest there is in military philately and specialisation is essential almost from the start. But very much of the material is still cheap and not hard to come by and the enthusiast can choose his speciality according to his pocket.

Plate 59 Spanish cover of 1939 with Isabella stamps of the new Nationalist Spain and the Nationalist frank with the portrait of Franco.

Paper Money, Posters and Leaflets

The collecting of banknotes has recently developed as a branch of coin collecting – a half-way house between numismatics and philately. The notes at present being sought are the early issues of U.K. banks. But as with all hobbies of this sort interest will widen. The moral is simple – collect military currency while the prices are still reasonable.

Money which has resulted from conditions of war has appeared in occupied territories, in besieged towns and in P.O.W. camps. Some of the best known siege money is that of Mafeking. The siege lasted 216 days, relief finally coming on Friday May 18th 1900. During the siege currency notes were issued by the authority of Colonel R. S. S. Baden Powell, commanding the Rhodesian Forces. The notes bore the words 'This voucher is good for the sum of . . . and will be exchanged for coin at Mafeking Branch of the Standard Bank on the resumption of Civil Law'.

During the First World War emergency notes were issued in France by Chambers of Commerce and Departments to make up for the shortage of coin, much of which was being used for paying allied forces. Le Havre, Rouen, Caen, Honfleur were some of the northern towns issuing notes while in the south a series came from the Region Provencale de Marseille with a map of the towns of the district on the reverse. A series also appeared in the German occupied areas of the Departments of Aisne, Ardennes and Marne. There were other issues for both occupied areas and French municipal centres. An outline of these is given by F. Philipson in the two articles in Coin Monthly (November and December 1972) French Emergency Notes of World War I.

During World War II notes were issued by British Military authority both in areas where troops were stationed in large numbers and in occupied territories. A fine series was issued for

North Africa and the Near East, lira notes were issued for Tripolitania and Italy and the list could be substantially extended. Japanese issues for territories occupied in the Far East are plentiful.

An interesting but scarcer collection of notes and substitutes for coinage appeared during the American Civil War. At first postage stamps were used for small change when coins became scarce, subsequently an ingenious salesman, John Gauet, hit on the idea of encasing these in mica to preserve them and make them more manageable. The use of stamps themselves was followed by small notes bearing reproductions of current stamps on them. Sticking stamps on cardboard discs was practised in the 1914–18 war and in the Spanish Civil War. Stamps used as currency are fairly common; frequently found are the Russian stamps of 1913 with instructions for their use as currency printed on the reverse.

An interesting class of notes is that of the concentration camps of the Nazi regime in Germany both before and during World War II. The camps differed in purpose and treatment but the following have been identified as issuing notes for the use of internees: Amersfoort (German camp established in the Netherlands), Auschvitz, Buchenwald, Dachau, Flossenburg, Gross-Rosen, Haselhorstnord, Litzmanstadt, Mauthausen, Nordhausen, Oranienburg, Ravensbruck, Sachenhausen, Stutthof, Theresienstadt, Vught, Westerbork. There were others in German occupied territory, including some in which notes were issued by the Vichy government.

Notes from some concentration camps are rare and may rise in price as high as £20 and more but the more common issues are available at around £2 a set. Sterling notes of the British Military Authority vary from four to six times face value. Lira notes are obtainable from about 50p and

Plate 60 For King and Country. A 'poster' given away with Answers magazine in October 1914.

For King and Country
(*How the 9th Lancers captured the guns in the Forest of Compiègne*)

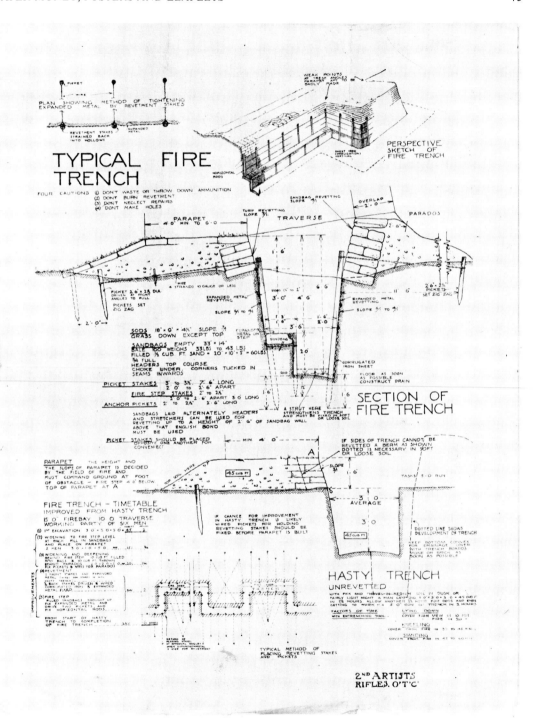

Plate 61 Training Leaflet for Trench Warfare. 2nd Artists' Rifles O.T.C. 1916.

Japanese occupation notes for even less.

Posters, proclamations, directions to the civil population, news broadsides, have all appeared in war time at least as early as the sixteenth century. Most of those which appear in bookseller's catalogues today relate to the period from the Crimea to the end of the last war. They fall into four main categories – recruitment, warnings and advice to the civil population, news items, directives from the civil or military authority. Among the recruitment posters is the famous 'Your country needs you' with the pointing hand of Kitchener driving home the message; pipe-smoking Tommy appears frequently expressing infinite self-confidence and happy satisfaction in his decision to serve his country; one such poster bears the rather optimistic caption 'The moment the order came to go forward, there were smiling faces everywhere'.

During World War II the civilian population was bombarded with warnings and reminders about gas masks, food economy, salvage of paper and metal for industry, the danger of idle talk and how to deal with incendiary bombs. Warnings about enemy attack were also issued in the form of official notices in World War I when naval bombardment was a constant hazard to coast towns. News via the poster was more common in the days when the newspaper only reached a relatively small part of the population. During the Crimean war broadsides appeared giving details of the latest telegraphic despatches from the theatre of war; these might be likened to the radio bulletins of World War II. Army unit notice boards often bore special news items from senior officers relevant to the unit or to a particular operation affecting the unit's activities or morale. Official notices appeared constantly in post-

Plate 62 Official Pamphlets of 1915 and 1939.

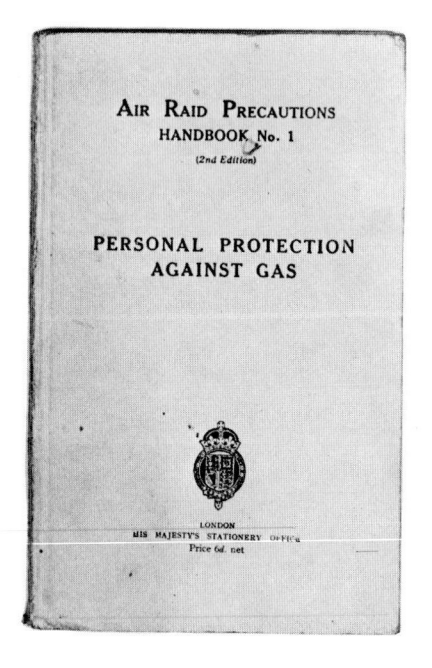

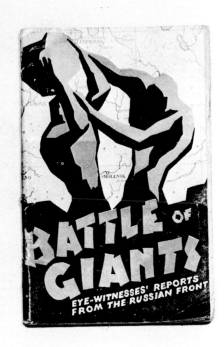

Plate 63 (*a*) & (*b*) Propaganda pamphlets.

offices, outside municipal buildings and elsewhere, relating to a host of topics from ration books to baby foods and how to draw allowances. These are truly the ephemera of wartime conditions and reflect the way in which the civil population were personally affected by events.

Prices

It is difficult to put prices to this material. Posters range around £5, but recently there has been a spate of reproductions of these posters and the collector needs to be on his guard. As with so much ephemera, the problem is rather to find it than how to pay for it. Booksellers' lists suggest that there is still quite a lot of this sort of material about priced between £2 and £5. A hunt in the cupboards of halls and public buildings used as clinics and canteens in the last war might well still reveal some interesting items.

Propaganda leaflets are a very different matter from the publicly displayed notice. Most of these leaflets or broadsides were dropped by air over enemy territory or clandestinely distributed by partisans or agents. To possess them endangered the life of the possessor and their immediate destruction either by the police or military reduced the number of them likely to survive. The purpose of these leaflets was to give news, usually backed by photographic evidence, in a way that would induce anxiety, distrust of authority, and lowering of morale.

These leaflets are now collected by a growing number of air history enthusiasts and appear in philatelic catalogues and auctions. The item illustrated on *Plate 63* was purchased at auction for £2.

Plate 64 War Songs of France and Germany.

Music, Concerts, Menus and Souvenirs

Music is included here because of the most attractive covers that appear on publications of nineteenth century music. The quadrille and its later version, the Lancers, were very popular dances from the early nineteenth century. The quadrille first became popular in France at the Court of Napoleon I and spread rapidly to England where it became a fashionable craze. One of the most prolific composers of quadrilles was Jullien who, sadly, in spite of making a fortune from his music, died a poverty stricken madman. Many pieces of dance music were published with attractive covers depicting soldiers in dress uniform, often in the romantic setting of the ballroom or garden of a stately home. These are sometimes in colour, sometimes black and white engravings. In their time they were precursors of the present imaginative photography that decorates the sleeves of gramophone records.

Songs as well as dances appeared in times of war and some attractive covers of the music that issued from the American Civil War have been seen illustrating in some detail the uniforms and types of the period. The Franco-Prussian war sparked off a new interest in the national songs of the contestants and is illustrated by the cover on *Plate 64*.

The band has always been a very popular part of peace-time military life and opportunities to perform were frequent. But not only the band would play a part of these occasions – singers and instrumentalists also had a role. The Smoking Concert was a popular regimental occasion and might include as many as forty items of songs, humorous recitations, instrumental solos as well as music from the band; the concert would go on until the early hours of the morning, sometimes it followed a dinner, an award of regimental prizes or other special occasion. The programmes for these concerts are of interest for several reasons, not only do they recall the songs and composers of the time, but trouble was taken to make them attractive and artists of considerable ability drew cartoons and sketches. A reunion dinner of 1920 was followed by a programme of music. 'Strube', later of *Daily Express* fame, illustrated in typical style L.Cpl. Pioneer (acting and unpaid) turns up 'with decorations'. The 'little man' of Strube's cartoons of the '20s and '30s is very recognisable in this sketch. Ernest Ibbetson drew for the covers of menus and concerts in serious and in light-hearted vein.

Many menus carry signatures of those present at the dinner and so constitute a unique record of personal interest, and such records deserve careful scrutiny for names that later became famous. A collection of menus and concert programmes of the Artists' Rifles in war and peace give an idea of eating habits. In 1904 dinner consisted of soup, filletted brill and lobster sauce, cutlets of mutton, saddle of mutton and jelly, roast beef, brussels sprouts and potatoes, rhubarb tart and cream, jelly, cheese and coffee. By 1916 the only noticeable change is that the main dish is more frequently game than roast. The Territorials were almost as much social clubs as military units; at a period when social life for any but the relatively wealthy was limited to the public house, service in the Territorial Army offered much that was enjoyable and was also a matter of considerable personal pride. Photographic souvenirs in the form of specially produced postcards and albums of photographs were produced to encourage enlistment and show 'a good life' in mess or in camp as well as on exercises and training. An attractive example by the 28th (County of London) Battalion, the London Regiment Artists' Rifles was produced in 1913 to commemorate two

periods of training under canvas, a week at
Abergavenny and a week in the Black Mountains.
The photographs were taken by the Commanding
Officer and others; the camp, meals, exercises, the
band, individual characters, the different cadres
of the regiment – scouts, signallers, cyclists, cooks,
transport and so on, are all shown in pleasingly
informal photographs; the collection is rounded
off with some interesting historic photographs of
the 1870s and 1880s.

Plate 65 Concert Programme and Greetings
Cards 1914-18.

Plate 66 Menus of 1909 by Ernest Ibbetson and R. B. Ogle.

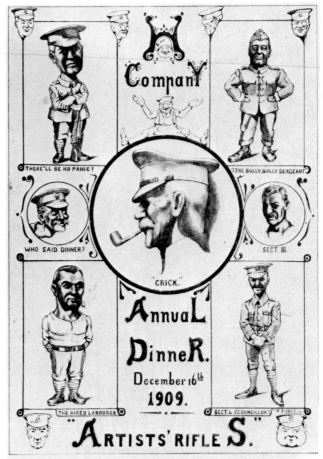

Notes on the Illustrations

Note on Frontispiece.
The Amir of Afghanistan in India. Grand Review of the Troops at Agra.
The Earl of Minto who is shown in the centre of the picture was Viceroy of India from 1905 to 1910 and was noted for the good relations that he established with the Indian princes. In the other roundels are shown to the left Their Highnesses the Maharajas of Nepal, Jodhpur, Indore and Mysore and to the right His Highness the Nizam of Hyderabad, the Gaekwar of Baroda, His Highness the Maharaja Sindhia of Gwalior and the Maharaja of Jammu and Kashmir.

Plate 1   (*a*) Cover from Durban to Prisoner of War Camp at Diyatalawa, Ceylon. The envelope has been opened and resealed with the adhesive label Opened Under Martial Law, and stamped with a Durban censor mark.

(*b*) Postcard from Sofia during the First Balkan War. (See notes on campaigns.) The correspondent (? a nurse) is on the way to Kirk-Kilisse where a hospital had been established under the auspices of the English Balkan Committee. Much of the work of this committee was due to Noel Buxton who aroused interest in England in the fate of the Balkan states which were seeking independence from Turkish rule. During the Balkan wars he recruited volunteers and raised money to establish hospitals in the war zones. The casualties at Kirk-Kilisse on October 24th 1912 were very heavy. The message is dated November 15th, but the Sophia cancellation is for November 2nd!

Plate 2   (*a*) Printed stationery envelope issued in 1879 for the use of the armed forces in India. This envelope is fairly common in mint condition, but is much scarcer when found used in campaigns outside India.

(*b*) Field Post envelope as used by German units in the period of the Franco-Prussian War.

Plates 3 & 4   Postal stationery used in Ruhleben Camp.
The Ruhleben race course near Berlin was opened in 1915 as an internment camp for British prisoners of war. About July the same year an internal postal service complete with locally printed cards, envelopes, letter-cards and stamps was organised by the prisoners. The R.X.D. or Ruhleben Express Delivery was operated until about May 1916 when it was suppressed by the German authorities. *Plate 3* shows a letter-card and an envelope produced in the camp. Since the camp was housed on a race course the prisoners occupied the stables, each of which had boxes downstairs and lofts above; access to the latter was by an outside staircase. Postboxes in each barrack were cleared six times a day and a similar number of deliveries was effected. An announcement in the camp magazine (see *Plate 45*) read "Why waste time rushing around the camp looking for

your friends? Drop a note in the R.X.D. letterboxes; it will only cost a ½d". Parcel post, registration and special delivery services were added to the normal postal services.

Plate 4 shows printed stationery in use after the suppression of the camp service. J. D. Ketchum has given a graphic account of life in this camp in his book *Ruhleben Camp, a Prison Camp Society* (1965).

Plate 5
: Printed stationery for use by Prisoners of War in Germany and a Field Postcard adapted for Prisoner of War use. World War I.

Plate 6
: British printed stationery for use by Prisoners of War in Great Britain during World War II.

Plate 7
(a) Cover used in World War II.
The Active Service Envelope, Army Form W3078. These were first issued in 1915 and were known as Privilege Envelopes. Up to the end of 1916 they were blue-green in colour without the cross design dividing the front. At about the end of 1916 the cross design appeared in heavy double green lines and the word ON was dropped leaving the heading ACTIVE SERVICE. The same design was used in World War II. In 1944 a newly designed envelope was produced divided down the centre but without the cross; this carried the title ACTIVE SERVICE with the additional words ARMY PRIVILEGE ENVELOPE above the left hand panel.

(b) German Air Field Post envelope with special air stamp issued on April 24th 1942. A clever forgery of this stamp was produced in Britain for personnel operating in German occupied territory.

Plate 8
: Field postcards from China despatched from Tientsin and Peking.
(a) The field post cancellation of the German Expeditionary Force under Field Marshal von Waldersee. (See notes on campaigns).
(b) Many cards from China at this period were attractively illustrated by hand painted scenes, flowers and figures. This seems to depict one of the Legation buildings in Legation Street, Peking. The front of this card carries an oval bilingual cancellation of Peking and a circular K. D. Feld. Postation No. 2.

Plate 9
: Illustrated postcards used by English and German troops during World War I.

Plate 10
: Postcards from the series "On Active Service by Air, Land and Sea" produced by Photochrom Co. Ltd., London and Tunbridge Wells.
(a) Behind the Sandbags.
(b) English soldiers escorting German prisoners for shipment to England. The first card has in the corner '£100 Prize'. Photographs taken at the front were very popular with the postcard producers and presumably this firm offered prizes for these, of which this was a winning one.

Plate 11
: *Daily Mail* Official War Pictures.
(a) One of Our Monster Guns.
(b) A London Heavy Battery in Action.

Plate 12
: Tributes to the much appreciated nursing profession.
(a) Au Revoir – not Good-Bye.
(b) A case for 'Blighty'.
The second card is a Canadian Official Photograph. The card is published by

		the *Daily Mirror* and printed by the Pictorial Newspaper Co. London.
Plate 13		Sentimental cards from England.
	(*a*)	My Heart's in my Homeland.

the *Daily Mirror* and printed by the Pictorial Newspaper Co. London.

Plate 13 Sentimental cards from England.

(*a*) My Heart's in my Homeland.
This card is produced by the firm of Bamforth and Co. who were founded by John Bamforth in 1870. They specialised in sentiment with songs, hymns and humorous verse.

(*b*) With my Love.
'It seems the world goes smoother,
And it kind of makes you smile,
When you know that though you're absent,
You're remembered all the while'.
This card has the message on the back 'To my dear soldier boy, with my love, Jess'.

Plates 14 & 15 Examples of sentiment from France. The expression of feeling is much the same, wishes of 'Good Luck' are frequent and the introduction of the child brings in an added element of pathos.

Plate 16 Italian – Second World War Card.

Plate 17 Humorous cards – First and Second World War.

Plates 18 & 19 Embroidered Cards. These very popular cards were produced sometimes with the miniature greeting card in the little silk envelope as illustrated in the first examples.

Plate 20 Propaganda cards produced in England.

Plate 21 (*a*) South African War Postcard.

(*b*) A Raphael Tuck 'Empire' postcard.

Plates 22 & 23 Postcards produced in France showing war damage and scenes of troop movements. Such cards as these were produced in large quantities for the use of the troops, many of them are of the 'before and after' sort. Most are now of little interest but those which depict scenes and weapons as well as notable buildings are worth retaining for the record.

Plate 24 (*a*) *Daily Mail* War Picture postcard.

(*b*) Official Photograph postcard.

Plate 25 Humorous cards by Tom Browne. Browne was born in Nottingham in 1870. He served an early apprenticeship to a firm of lithographers and learned to draw with considerable skill. He turned his attention to humorous work early in his career and drew for Tatler and Punch. He exhibited at the Royal Academy in 1897 and produced Tom Browne's Comic Annual in 1904. He died in 1910.

Plate 26 Fragments from France. By Captain Bruce Bairnsfather. The very popular cartoons of Bruce Bairnsfather, creator of "Old Bill", appeared during World War I in the Bystander and the collected volume illustrated here contains a preface by the Editor of that magazine. The cartoons were humorous but had a serious side to which the Editor draws attention; "If this sketchbook is worthy to outlast the days of the war, and to be kept for remembrance on the shelves of those who have lived through it, it will have done its bit. For will it not be a standing reminder of the ingloriousness of war, its preposterous absurdity, and of its futility as a means of settling the affairs of nations".

Bruce Bairnsfather was born in India of a military family. He was educated at the United Services College, Westward Ho and became a civil engineer. He joined the Royal Warwickshire Militia and went to France with the 1st Warwickshire Regiment. He became a Captain in 1915 and served at the front until the end of 1916 when he was transferred to the War Office. In August 1917 he produced a play 'The Better 'Ole' in collaboration with Captain A. Eliot. He also wrote *Bullets and Billetts* and *From Mud to Mufti*.

Plate 27   Notes and Reminiscenses of a Staff Officer by Lieutenant-Colonel Basil Jackson. This is a presentation copy of this privately printed book to the author's granddaughter, together with a photograph of a painting of the field of Waterloo after the battle, by Anne de la Tour. Jackson served at Waterloo and later on St. Helena.

Plate 28   (*a*) A Voice from Waterloo by Sergeant Major E. Cotton. 1849. Another of Lieutenant-Colonel Jackson's books. He has written on the fly-leaf "We have many accounts of the battle of Waterloo by writers of greater pretension than the author of this little book. Mr Cotton has taken infinite pains to be correct in his statements, and in general they may be relied upon. B. J". He adds "I cannot say much in praise of the portraits".

At page 21 (here illustrated) the author writes "The first hint to Picton of the Duke's intention to retreat was an order conveyed to him, to collect his wounded; when he growled out, with his Stentorian voice 'Very well, sir' in a tone that showed his reluctance to quit the ground his troops had so bravely maintained the day before".

Jackson has added the footnote to this paragraph: "I carried this message and certainly it vexed him much. B.J".

(*b*) The *Diary* of a V.A.D. nurse.

Plates 29 & 30   Thomas Beale Cooper, to whom these Commissions were granted, was appointed
(*see also Plate 34*)   Lieutenant in a Company of the Regiment of Militia of the County of Warwick in 1796 (*Plate 34*). The defence of England against the possible attack of Napoleon's army was in the hands of a small and inadequately trained army of less than 40,000 regulars and about 50,000 militia. Against this Napoleon's grand army numbered 160,000. During 1803 and 1804 great efforts were made to increase this force by the creation of a new body of volunteers to be known as the Supplementary Militia. Cooper was duly appointed a Lieutenant in a Battalion of the Supplementary Militia of the County of Warwick in 1803 (see *Plate 29*) and was appointed Paymaster on August 27th 1803. A further series of documents (not illustrated here) enables us to show the changes in organisation that the pressures of the Napoleonic wars brought upon the army. In 1807 Cooper transferred to the Worcestershire Militia under an Act passed "in the forty seventh year of His Majesty's Reign intituled 'An Act for Amending the Laws relating to the Militia in England and for augmenting the Militia' " and on September 24th the following year under "an Act of Parliament passed in the forty eighth year of His present Majesty's Reign intituled 'An Act for enabling His Majesty to establish a permanent Local Militia under certain restrictions for the Defence of the Realm'". Cooper was appointed Major in the East Worcester Regiment of the Local Militia. In 1809 he was appointed Lieutenant-Colonel of the Regiment.

In 1817, after the wars were over, he was appointed Lieutenant-Colonel Commandant "but not to take rank in the Army except during the time of the said corps being called out into actual service".

The home defence force that was raised in 1803–4 was considerable in number but very inefficient in terms of training and weapons. It was largely due to the work of Robert Stewart, Viscount Castlereagh, who was appointed to War and Colonial Office by Pitt in 1805, that by 1808 the local militia was 65,000 strong, a well trained and effective force.

Plate 31   Memorial scroll for a Midshipman killed in the First World War.

Plate 32   (*a*)   A letter from France dated June 28th 1791.

"Dear Sir,
I began to write to you last week about some of the details of our revolutions and the flight of the king who was thought already to be off French soil, but the false news that he had been arrested persuaded me to put off making you a part of all this uncertain news; now, sir, his arrest is confirmed; he has been arrested at Varennes as we learn from the letters set out below, and was subsequently taken to Paris".

This letter was written very near the events recorded. The King made an attempt to reach the Austrians at the frontier town of Montmedy. But the plan was badly executed and the arrest of the King and the royal family was effected at Varennes. They were brought back to Paris on June 25th.

The recipient of this letter has noted the time and date at which he received it namely July 1st in the morning. We could scarcely do better today.

(*b*)   A contemporary letter describing celebrations at Evesham on the victory of the allies at Leipzig in October 1813. The cautious comment continues "Bonaparte has a most inventive mind and has still vast resources left – enough for half a dozen campaigns."

Plate 33   (*a*)   Uniform list for a cadet in the Royal Regiment of Artillery at Woolwich who completed his course of training in 1816.

(*b*)   A letter of 1816 from the above-mentioned officer describing an exercise with Congreve rockets. He writes:

". . . they went off on the whole much better than usual owing to 2 causes, first the stick being screwed into the centre of the rocket instead of being fixed as it formerly was to the side, and secondly their being fired through a long tube so constructed as to give them the requisite elevation instead of being laid in a trough, the old mode of firing them. They are however capable of much improvement, the stick not being supported when they are laid in the above-mentioned tube, this gives them a zig-zag motion which the tube is not long enough to prevent; the only effect that you can depend upon is that they will most assuredly frighten the horses of those who fire them in their present state. I would much sooner have a brigade of heavy 6 pounders with shrapnel shells and canister shot".

The Congreve rocket was the result of experiments carried out at Woolwich in the 1780s by William Congreve. The first operational rocket appeared in 1805 and they were used in the bombardment of Boulogne in 1806 and of Copenhagen in 1807. But they were dangerous to fuse and were not accurate for the reasons stated in the letter. Several sizes and mountings were tried out, but the Artillery did not like them.

Plate 34	Appointment to a Lieutenancy in the Warwickshire militia. (See *Plates 29 & 30*).
Plate 35	Passport of Rowland Hughes – September 1870, admitting him to France.

Below is an envelope addressed to Hughes while he was in France from which we see that he had joined the Legion of the Friends of France. He was in Paris during the siege of the city by the Prussian army. (See notes on Campaigns.)

Plate 36 — Laissez-Passer with which Hughes left Paris in February 1871. It is printed in both German and French. He was only 20 at the time and other letters reveal that he was in the city to secure a post with a merchant to whom he had previously written. His applications for the post were written in both French and German which he spoke fluently.

Plate 37 — The Black and White Budget.

This magazine first appeared as the Black and White Transvaal Special in September 1899 and as the Black and White Budget the following month. It appeared every Friday, price 6d and was published by the Black and White Publishing Company Limited of Fleet Street. It presented a detailed photographic record of the war in South Africa with a limited letter press of notes and articles on a variety of topics. It interspersed the photographs with art work and kept up a useful and detailed Diary of Events.

Plate 38		Red Cross and St. John's awards presented to a nursing sister 1919.
Plate 39		Personal documents on discharge 1920 and allowance instructions for the wife of a newly commissioned officer.
Plate 40	(*a*)	Pay Book and Release Book 1939–45.
	(*b*)	Uniform list from military tailor 1917.
Plate 41–42		Photographs from personal collections.
Plate 43	(*a*)	Artists' Rifles *c*. 1890–95.
	(*b*)	Petersfield Camp 1908.
	(*c*)	'B' Company 1913.

An interesting record of changing uniforms.

Plate 44 — The Bristol Mercury of August 1815 with report of an interview with Napoleon at Plymouth when he was transferred from the 'Bellerophon' to the 'Northumberland' which was to take him to St. Helena.

Plate 45	Ruhleben Camp Magazine. (See Plates 3–4).
Plate 46	Belgian newspaper – L'Indépendance Belge – produced in London for the numerous Belgian refugees who came to England after their country was overrun by the German army.
Plate 47	Evening News for Armistice Day 1918.
Plate 48	News Sheet dropped by the R.A.F. in advance of allied troops. August 1944.
Plate 49	Halifax Garrison Artillery. The Artillery at this date (c. 1900) was divided into the Horse, Field and Garrison Artillery. The latter were frequently employed on coastal defence.
Plate 50	The Cape Mounted Rifles. This corps was formed in 1878 from the Frontier Armed and Mounted Police and became the 1st Regiment South African

	Mounted Rifles in 1913. Both these Plates (49–50) are chromolithographs by H. Bunnet.
Plate 51 & 52	Photographic illustrations from L. Creswicke: South Africa and the Transvaal War. These rather uninspiring plates have the merit of accuracy. The book, in seven volumes, was published in 1900 and contains many spirited and artistic drawings of troops in action as well as photographs of uniforms and equipment.
Plate 53	Christmas cards of World War I.
Plate 54	Cigarette Cards depicting military uniform, head-dress, medals, and regimental badges and standards. The cards illustrated are all from John Player of Nottingham, except the Maharajah Sir Pertab Singhji who comes from a series of Allied Army Leaders by W. D. and H. O. Wills of Bristol and Trooper Morris V.C. who figures among V.C. Heroes by Taddy's Premier Navy Cut.
Plate 55	Raising a loan to buy out an officer of the Regiment in order to gain promotion. All those junior officers affected joined in the contract.
Plate 56	Welcome Home to troops returning from South Africa. November 1900.
Plate 57	Stamps of Great Britain used in South Africa during the Boer War. The cancellations are of the British Army Field Post Office, the Army Post Office, and the town cancellations of Bethulie, Kimberley and Belmont.
Plate 58	Commemorative folder to President Dr E. Benes on his 57th birthday by the Czechoslovak Army and Air Force in Great Britain, 28th May 1941. One thousand copies of this tribute were issued bearing appropriately the stamps of 1919 depicting the lion breaking free from his chains issued by Czechoslovakia on the first anniversary of Independence. A tribute to the President's work for Czechoslovakia and a quotation from one of his speeches made to army units after the collapse of France are set out on the page facing the commemorative stamps.
Plate 59	Spanish cover of 1939 with Isabella stamps of the new Nationalist Spain and the Nationalist frank with the portrait of Franco. During the Spanish Civil War a large number of special stamps and markings of all sorts for censorship, propaganda, political allegiance and other uses were produced by both sides; these are fully described and illustrated in R. G. Shelley, *The Postal History of the Spanish Civil War 1936-1939.*
Plate 60	For King and Country. A 'poster' given away with *Answers* magazine in October 1914. The artist, Ernest Ibbetson, was a popular postcard artist and was working for Gale and Polden on military themes early in the century.
Plate 61	Training Leaflet for Trench Warfare. 2nd Artists' Rifles O.T.C. 1916.
Plate 62	Official Pamphlets of 1915 and 1939.
Plate 63	Propaganda pamphlets.
(*a*)	1945.
(*b*)	Undated but refers to the first six weeks of fighting on the Russian Front.
Plate 64	*War Songs of France and Germany.* English versions of the songs are supplied by H. B. Farnie. The collection contains: The German Fatherland, The Watch by the Rhine. The Blucher Song. Thou Shalt Not Have It. The Marseillaise. For Native Country Dying. French Marching Song. Parisian War Song.
Plate 65	Concert Programme and Greetings Cards 1914–18.
Plate 66	Menus of 1909 by Ernest Ibbetson and R. B. Ogle.

Notes on Campaigns 1809-1913

The notes that follow are only indications of date and geography of localised campaigns that may suggest some sources of material for the collector. For more detailed information reference should be made to the list of useful books and addresses at the end of the volume.

PENINSULAR WAR 1809–1813

The war was the result of an attempt to encourage Portuguese and Spanish resistance to Napoleon. Sir Arthur Wellesley, later Duke of Wellington, was in command at the beginning of the war and defeated the French at Vimiera. He was succeeded by Sir John Moore who was killed at Corunna in January 1809. Wellesley returned to a victory at Talavera in July 1809. Further victories over the French followed at Salamanca in July 1812, Vittoria in June 1813, and Toulouse in April 1814.

ANGLO-AMERICAN WAR OF 1812–14

War began on June 18th 1812. American land forces attacked Canada from Detroit and at Niagara and Lake Champlain. In April 1813 Toronto was attacked. In 1814 British troops landed at Chesapeake Bay; Washington was occupied on 24–25 August. There were several naval engagements during the war including that between H.M.S. *Shannon* and U.S.S. *Chesapeake* in which the latter was captured. Peace was concluded in December 1814.

SIKH WARS (1) 1845–46

The army took over after the death of Ranjit Singh. On December 11th 1845 the Sikhs crossed the Sutlej river and Britain declared war on the 13th. In the same month, in spite of fierce fighting by the Sikhs the British, under Sir Hugh Gough, scored victories at Moodkee near Ferozepore and at Ferozeshuhur in the central Punjab. Two further victories by the British in January 1846 at Aliwal and Sobraon resulted in the British occupation of Lahore. In the peace terms that followed in February the Sikhs ceded Kashmir to Britain in addition to a heavy fine imposed on them.

SIKH WARS (2) 1848–49

On April 20th 1848 two British officers were murdered and a local Sikh revolt developed in South West Punjab. The neighbouring Afghans were drawn in on the Sikh side. Gough advanced into the Punjab and attacked the Sikhs at Ramnagar in the North West. The outcome was indecisive and a second engagement took place on January 13th 1849 at Chilianwala. On February 21st 1849 both Sikhs and Afghans were defeated at Goojerat and the Punjab was annexed to Britain on March 30th 1849.

CRIMEAN WAR 1853–56

The initial cause of the war was the Turkish reluctance to protect the Christians of the Turkish Empire, but a more deeply laid reason was Britain's fear that Russia was about to partition the Turkish Empire in her own interests. The Turks declared war on September 23rd 1853 and their fleet was destroyed at Sinope on November 30th. War broke out between Britain and France and Russia in March 1854. In September landings were effected in the Crimea and Sebastapol was besieged until September 1855. On October 25th 1854 the Russians attacked the British at Balaclava and were repulsed by the Highlanders and the Cavalry. The charge of the Light Brigade under Lord Cardigan took place in the course of this battle. The battle of Inkerman followed on November 5th when the Russians tried to break through the British lines; Russian losses were 12,000 killed, captured or wounded. It was at the end of October 1854 that Florence Nightingale went to Scutari to nurse the sick and wounded from the Crimean battlefields.

The war ended on February 1st 1856 and final terms were concluded at the Congress of Paris in February and March.

AMERICAN CIVIL WAR 1861–65

The immediate cause of war between the slave owning south and the industrialised north was the attack by Confederacy troops upon the Federal garrison at Fort Sumter on April 12th 1861. Lincoln raised a volunteer force to suppress the rising and military operations began in June. On July 21st Thomas J. Jackson defeated the Union forces at Bull Run, Virginia and scored a second victory in August 1862; Robert E. Lee continued to make gains for the Confederates in early 1863 but was defeated at Gettysburg (July 1–3) by General George C. Meade. This was the scene of Lincoln's famous speech. The Unionists lost 3,000 and the Confederates 4,000 in this three day battle. In the same year Ulysses S. Grant, later to become President, scored decisive Unionist victories at Vicksburg and Chattanooga and became commander of the Union forces in March 1864. In the summer of 1864 William T. Sherman invaded Georgia and in the winter drove a wedge through the South and split the Confederate territory. Lee surrendered at Appomattox on April 9th 1865. Lincoln was assassinated on April 14th and Sherman accepted the final surrender of Confederate troops on April 26th.

FRANCO-PRUSSIAN WAR 1870–71

The cause of the war was rivalry between the North German Confederation and French Second Empire for European dominance. The immediate cause was the Ems Telegram of July 13th 1870 in which it was made to appear that the French Ambassador and the King of Prussia had exchanged mutual insults. The text of the original telegram had been altered by Bismarck to give this impression. France declared war on Prussia on July 19th. During August the French army suffered defeats on the eastern border which culminated in the battle of Sedan on September 1st at which Napoleon III was captured. The French Army was again defeated at Metz in October and Paris was besieged from September 19th to January 28th 1871. Peace was finally agreed on March 1st. Alsace and Lorraine were ceded to Germany and the Treaty of Frankfurt was signed on May 10th 1871.

AFGHAN WARS

Fighting on the Afghan frontier was a constant occupation for British troops in India but there were two periods of war which were related chiefly to the need to ensure British influence in a buffer region between India and Russia.

(1) 1838–1842

A long drawn out campaign in which George Eden, first Earl of Auckland attempted to reduce Afghanistan to British vassalage by deposing the Amir Dost Mohammad and replacing him by Shah Shuja. But though the British occupied Kabul for two years they were defeated in November 1841 with heavy casualties.

(2) 1878–1881

This was triggered by the refusal of the British to give aid to the Amir Sher Ali in his struggle for internal support; he turned to Russia as the alternative power and accepted a Russian mission at Kabul. The British immediately sent an envoy but he was turned back at the frontier. Britain therefore declared war in November 1878. By May 1879 Roberts had secured a treaty but remained in position to ensure its implementation (Treaty of Gundamuck). This was not the end of the affair and subsequent risings compelled Roberts to occupy Kabul. Negotiations eventually secured the accession of Abaur Rahman to the Emirate and British forces finally left Afghan territory in April 1881. It was in this later campaign that Roberts marched from Kabul to Kandahar – 320 miles in 23 days.

THE EGYPTIAN WARS OF 1882 and 1896

The first engagement in Egypt was the result of nationalist revolt under one of the colonels of the native army – Arabi Pasha. The Turkish government refused to take any action against the nationalist forces and France withdrew at the last moment because of the fall from office of Gambetta. Gladstone, with some reluctance, decided to act. A bombardment of Alexandria by the British fleet in June 1882 was followed by the landing of army units under the command of Sir Garnet Wolseley. Arab forces were eventually defeated the following September at Tel-el-Kebir after elaborate preparations by the British.

In 1883 Sir Evelyn Baring, later Lord Cromer, was sent to Egypt to achieve some degree of settlement and stability. One of his first tasks was to extricate the Egyptian army from the Sudan in order to reform and retrain it. For this task General Charles Gordon was chosen. Instead of getting the army out he attempted to defeat the Mahdi and established himself at Khartoum. Here he was besieged and eventually killed.

It was not until 1896 that Sir Herbert Kitchener, after Cromer had restored the finances and army of Egypt, marched into the Sudan and defeated the Mahdi at Omdurman outside Khartoum and so avenged Gordon's death.

BURMA WAR 1885

Burma was annexed to Britain in three stages. First in 1824 when Rangoon was captured, then in 1852 when the Irrawaddy Delta was annexed and finally in 1885 when King Theebaw seized the Bombay–Burma Company property. The King was seized in his capital. Mandalay and the Burmese army made no effective resistance. It took several years, however, to establish peace in the province and it was not until 1894 that the country settled down.

ASHANTI WARS (1) 1873–74

The tribes of the Gold Coast, in the course of the inter-tribal disputes, came into contact with the British garrison at Elmina on the coast near the mouth of the river Pra. Their persistent harassing of the garrison was considered sufficiently serious to send a force under Viscount Wolseley to lead an offensive campaign against the Ashanti tribe. He crossed the Pra river and pressed on to Kumasi in spite of King Coffee Kalkalli's request for peace. Kumasi was destroyed.

(2) 1895–96

King Prempeh, Coffee's successor, refused to accept the terms that had been imposed by the previous campaign. A further attack on Kumasi was launched without much opposition and a British residency established.

(3) 1900

A more serious expedition was necessary to relieve a siege of Kumasi. This was led by Col. James Willcocks and resulted in the final annexation of Ashanti.

BOER WAR 1899–1902

The war was the result of the colonial policy of Chamberlain and the attack by Kruger, with German arms, on Cape Colony and Natal in September 1899.

The war began on October 11th with Boer successes and the sieges of Ladysmith, Mafeking and Kimberley. Kitchener and Roberts came to Africa in January 1900, and under their command British fortunes changed. Kimberley was relieved on February 15th 1900 after 123 days siege, Ladysmith followed on the 28th after 120 days and finally Mafeking, which was defended by Baden Powell, was relieved on May 18th after 216 days. On June 5th Roberts occupied Pretoria, and the Transvaal was annexed in September.

The second stage of the war from September 1900 to the Treaty of Vereeniging on May 31st. 1902 was a period of guerilla war. During this time the British erected blockhouses to defend railways and roads and, as time went on, to divide the country into manageable areas. At the same time population sympathetic to the Boers and on whom they relied for help and shelter were removed and put into concentration camps where conditions were often very poor. By the final peace Britain granted self-government to the Union of Boer Republics.

BOXER RISING 1900

The acquisition of the Treaty ports of China by the European imperial powers aroused considerable anti-European feeling in Northern China. The 'Boxers' were a secret society which existed with the tacit support of the Imperial government. Their attacks were directed against European missionaries and the employees of European commercial enterprises. It was decided that it was essential to defend European nationals and Admiral Sir E. H. Seymour attempted a relief expedition in June directed towards Peking. The

Boxers retaliated by an outbreak in Peking itself; on June 19th the German minister was assassinated and the foreign legations were besieged. They were relieved on August 14th and a German Expeditionary force was sent out under General von Waldersee to avenge the assassination and prevent further risings. The methods of repression employed by the imperial powers were stern and drove the nationalists into the movement later headed by Sun Yat Sen.

THE EXPEDITION TO TIBET 1904

In 1903 attempts had been made to open up Tibet to trade. There was also an anxiety lest Russia should endanger the northern frontier of India by gaining influence over the Tibetans. An expedition was therefore despatched under Sir Francis Younghusband and in April 1904 they reached Gyangtse. The Tibetans resisted this incursion into their territory, but eventually a small contingent reached Lhasa and made a satisfactory treaty with the Dalai Llama. They returned to India in October.

RUSSO-JAPANESE WAR 1904–5

Russia and Japan were both seeking influence in Manchuria and Korea. The Japanese attacked the Russian fleet in Port Arthur on February 8th 1904. The Russian fleet's attempt to sail from the Baltic to Japan ended in disaster and defeat at Tsushima in May 1905. America mediated between the contestants and peace was signed in September 1905.

BALKAN WARS 1912–13

These two wars were the outcome of nationalist feeling in the Balkan states which were under Turkish rule and the centralised policy of the Turkish government which refused to grant concessions to the Christian populations of Macedonia and Thrace. The attack on Turkey by Italy in 1911 gave the opportunity for the Balkan states to take joint action. By October 1912 Bulgaria, Serbia, Greece and Montenegro had formed the Balkan League. War began on October 18th and the Turks were heavily defeated at Kirk-Kilisse on October 22–23rd, and at Lule-Burgas on October 29–31st. Both these were Bulgarian victories. At the same time attacks were made by the Serbs at Kumanovo and by the Montenegrins at Scutari. An independent state of Albania was declared on November 28th and an armistice was signed on December 3rd.

The Balkan League soon fell apart and on June 27th 1913 Bulgarians marched into Roumanian territory; at the same time the Turks retook Adrianople in Thrace. The Bulgarians were faced with the Roumanian army and with the Turks at their rear. Their position was hopeless and the Treaty of Bucharest was signed on August 10th 1913. Events and alliances springing from this treaty and the position in which it placed the European powers laid the scene for the opening of the Great War of 1914–18.

Some Useful Books and Addresses

Prints and Pictures

Carman W. Y.	British Military Uniforms from Contemporary Pictures. 1957.
Gunn M. J.	Print Restoration and Picture Cleaning. 1911.
Neville R.	British Military Prints. 1909.

Postal History

Clement A.	Kleines Handbuch der Deutschen Feldpost. 2 vols.
Fladung E. (Ed.)	Priced Catalogue of Postal Stationery of the World. Published in loose-leaf form with binders alphabetically by Higgins and Gage Inc. California U.S.A. (usually referred to by the name of the publishers).
Huggins A. K.	British Postal Stationery. G. B. Philatelic Society. London 1970.
Raynor P. E.	A Reference List of British Army Postmarks used in the Great War 1914–19.
Shelley R. G.	The Postal History of the Spanish Civil War 1936–39.
Tranmer K.	Austro-Hungarian Military Post 1914–18.

Philatelic literature is supplied by some of the larger booksellers and from specialists such as Harris Publications Ltd., 42 Maiden Street, Strand, London; Vera Trinder Ltd., 38 Bedford Street, Strand, London.

Postcards

Holt T. and V.	Picture Postcards of the Golden Age. 1971.
Staff F.	The Picture Postcard and its Origins. 1966.

Lists obtainable from: International Postcard Market, 96 Idmiston Road, West Norwood, London. See also the Exchange and Mart published weekly and available from newsagents.

Newspapers

Bourne H. R. F.	English Newspapers. 2 vols. 1887.
Robbins Sir A.	The Press. 1928.

Stamps

The relevant literature is mostly in the form of articles in the periodicals: Gibbons Stamp Monthly, The Stamp Magazine (monthly), Stamp Collecting Weekly. These are all available at most newsagents and the names and addresses of suppliers may be found in them.

The best catalogues for the collector are those supplied by Stanley Gibbons Ltd., 391 Strand, London and Scott's Standard Postage Stamp Catalogue (3 vols.) published by Scott Publishing Co., 604 Fifth Avenue, New York.

Money

Narbeth C.	How to collect Paper Money. Published by Arthur Barker, 5 Winsley Street, London.

Lists available from: David Keable, 37 Godstone Road, Purley, Surrey. See also Coin Monthly, and Coins. Several of the leading philatelic dealers also deal in paper money.

General Ephemera, etc.

Catalogues from Jabez Elliott Ltd., 9 Hampstead High Street, London. See also advertisers in Times Literary Supplement.

Books

The following are now out of print but may be found in libraries and in second-hand book shops.
They are useful for those particularly interested in the campaign they cover:

Cassell's History of the War between France and Germany. 2 vols.

Creswicke L. South Africa and the Transvaal War. 7 vols. 1901.

Nolan E. H. History of the War against Russia. 1857.

The following will be found useful for general reference and are all at present in print at reasonable prices.

Barnes R. M.	A History of the Regiments and Uniforms of the British Army. Military Uniforms of Britain and the Empire. (Sphere Books Ltd.)
Bond B.	Victorian Military Campaigns. 1967.
Calder A.	The People's War. Panther Books.
Collier B.	A Short History of the Second World War. Fontana.
Ffrench Blake R. L. V.	The Crimean War. Sphere Books Ltd.
Gilbert M.	Recent History Atlas. First World War Atlas. Weidenfeld and Nicholson.
Johnson D. E.	Collecting Militaria. Arthur Barker.
Jones B. and Howell B.	Popular Arts of the First World War. Studio Vista. (This book gives illustrations of much of the ephemera of World War I. It is designed for the interest of the art forms rather than for the collector but it contains much information that is very useful).
Pemberton W. B.	Battles of the Boer War. Pan Books.
Taylor A. J. P.	The First World War. An illustrated history. Penguin.
Wilkinson F.	Militaria. Ward Lock.

Lists of military books may be obtained from the following booksellers:

Victor Sutcliffe, The Old School, Asthal, Burford, Oxford.

Peter H. Taylor, 162 Sycamore Road, Farnborough, Hants.

Forces Postal History

Information about the Society may be obtained from the Secretary:

W. Garrard, 7 Hillbeck Way, Greenford, Middlesex.